JESUS
OVER

———

EVERY
THING

JESUS OVER
EVERY
THING

UNCOMPLICATING THE DAILY
STRUGGLE TO PUT JESUS FIRST

LISA WHITTLE

W PUBLISHING GROUP

AN IMPRINT OF THOMAS NELSON

Jesus over Everything
© 2020 Lisa Whittle

Published in Nashville, Tennessee, by W Publishing Group, an imprint of Thomas Nelson.

The author is represented by Alive Literary Agency, www.aliveliterary.com.

Thomas Nelson titles may be purchased in bulk for educational, business, fund-raising, or sales promotional use. For information, please e-mail SpecialMarkets@ThomasNelson.com.

Unless otherwise indicated, Scripture quotations are taken from the Holy Bible, New Living Translation. © 1996, 2004, 2007, 2013, 2015 by Tyndale House Foundation. Used by permission of Tyndale House Publishers, Inc., Carol Stream, Illinois 60188. All rights reserved.

Scripture quotations marked CSB are taken from The Christian Standard Bible. © 2017 by Holman Bible Publishers. Used by permission. Christian Standard Bible®, and CSB® are federally registered trademarks of Holman Bible Publishers.

Scripture quotations marked ESV are taken from the ESV® Bible (The Holy Bible, English Standard Version®), © 2001 by Crossway, a publishing ministry of Good News Publishers. Used by permission. All rights reserved.

Scripture quotations marked HCSB are taken from the Holman Christian Standard Bible®, © 1999, 2000, 2002, 2003, 2009 by Holman Bible Publishers. Used by permission. HCSB® is a federally registered trademark of Holman Bible Publishers.

Scripture quotations marked KJV are taken from the Holy Bible, King James Version (public domain).

Scripture quotations marked THE MESSAGE are taken from The Message. © by Eugene H. Peterson 1993, 1994, 1995, 1996, 2000, 2001, 2002. Used by permission of NavPress. All rights reserved. Represented by Tyndale House Publishers, Inc.

Scripture quotations marked NIV are taken from the Holy Bible, New International Version®, NIV®. © 1973, 1978, 1984, 2011 by Biblica, Inc.® Used by permission of Zondervan. All rights reserved worldwide.

Scripture quotations marked NKJV are taken from the New King James Version®. © 1982 by Thomas Nelson. Used by permission. All rights reserved.

Scripture quotations marked TPT are taken from The Passion Translation®. © 2017 by BroadStreet Publishing® Group, LLC. Used by permission. All rights reserved.

Any Internet addresses, phone numbers, or company or product information printed in this book are offered as a resource and are not intended in any way to be or to imply an endorsement by Thomas Nelson, nor does Thomas Nelson vouch for the existence, content, or services of these sites, phone numbers, companies, or products beyond the life of this book.

ISBN 978-0-7852-3199-8 (eBook)

Library of Congress Control Number: 2019046956

ISBN 978-0-7852-3198-1 (TP)

Printed in the United States of America

20 21 22 23 24 LSC 10 9 8 7 6 5 4 3 2 1

For my Truest Love since I was six

CONTENTS

ONE

THE LAND OF THE DEADLY *OVERS*

WE ARE BORN HOMESICK, EVERY ONE OF US.
—LORE WILBERT

As long as I can remember, I've been hungry for a simpler life.

Enter Enid, Oklahoma, the home of my splintery tree fort, brown paneled-wall country home, venison Crock-Pot cook-offs, and the last place I remember life not feeling like a raging list of to-dos. I was about six, maybe seven. I ran in the grass and held stray kittens for a living, without knowing about catching the dreaded ringworm. (I eventually found out.) Daddy preached in the big church in town, and Mom did basically everything else, so far as I could see.

It's not that the years that followed brought monumental snags. It's that those years of holding kittens are the last *I can remember* feeling completely carefree. Preteen angst shortly took over. Awareness of people not keeping their word. And the life juggle in general that requires priority lists. I've always been a list queen, with the hopes of keeping it all straight. Interesting how people I know who live by these lists claim they bring us the sanity that they secretly steal from us.

And then there's Jesus.

He's a large part of my simpler life story and my list story too: the fifth member of the Reimer family, woven in between Daddy, Mom, older brother Mark, and me during those blessed early years. (The deer carcasses hanging in the garage don't count since they contributed only to the cook-offs, and my little sister wasn't born yet.) Unlike my brother and me, with our personalized rooms, Jesus got free rein over every room in the house but lived especially in the big white Bible on the coffee table and, since I was six, inside of me. I grasped this concept because my parents explained it to me, and I believed it for myself since it was something I accepted, received, and, subsequently, felt. Our family loved Him—both my parents, in their own way, made sure. I loved Him. My whole life I have.

> Interesting how people I know who live by these lists claim they bring us the sanity that they secretly steal from us.

But I also love me. Sometimes I love me more. This is where things get complicated.

Forty years later and it remains the story of my life.

ME OVER JESUS

A few years ago I did something long overdue: I went on a one-year shopping fast.

I wish I could say I did it because I wanted to. I would prefer to spin this with me looking spiritual and disciplined. But the truth is I did it because one day God nudged me into it by good old-fashioned embarrassment.

I'll tell you about that. But first, let's go back.

My expression through clothes came early for me as a little girl—my mom told me so, and I've seen it myself in pictures: the cool, strapless clogs with striped, mismatched Dorrie-esque socks (yes, *that* Dorrie from the library books) with the floral, off-the-shoulder dress for an attempt at eclecticism (close but no cigar). Then came those wide teenage belts and funky MC Hammer pants and all that unapologetic '80s flair as I got older. I found no suitable prom dresses to fit my style, so I had my mom make them.

Clothes, even to this day, make me feel like my most authentic me. Putting them together: an art. Wearing what I want no matter the rules: a rebellion. I find particular pleasure in buying clothes on a budget—looking like I pay far more for things than I actually have. It has become a bit of a game to me in my adulthood—from my clothes to my home décor—feeling joy over how many times I can secure wide-eyed compliments like *You paid what? No way. That looks too good.* Like the brown-and-silver vases I purchased from Publix at $12.99 apiece when my kids were mere babies, the ones that sat on my mantel for years. My heart leaped every time I heard the words, "You mean the grocery store Publix?" I'd grown so fond of my talent in shopping over the years. It had become a trusted and dear friend.

So when God began to talk to me about how shopping had gotten too high on my priority list, I balked at the ludicrous suggestion.

I don't buy expensive things. I have not and do not put our family into debt. For twenty years, up until a few months ago when it became a work necessity, I didn't even own a credit card. It felt ridiculous to think of shopping as a problem for me or for God. I was worshipping Him, loving Him, doing full-time ministry for Him. I felt like He should let me have this one.

We stayed at a stalemate.

Life went on, and I flew to Honduras to serve God some more. I spoke to a crowded roomful of people with a Spanish interpreter—kissed the cheek of a woman who was days away from dying with cancer with no meds to ease the raging pain inside her bones. I wrapped my favorite necklace around the neck of a local woman who could speak to me only through her eyes and hugged her tight enough to say "I love you" with my arms. *See me loving You most, God?* I thought, in the quiet of my mind. *See how I'm not bound by my love for things and can even give up my favorite necklace? See how You are over all of my life?* I felt proud of myself for all the ways I was putting Jesus at the top of my list.

I came back home to the US to a waiting family, a warm bed, and a full closet, which dug at me a little after the poverty I'd just seen. But I wasn't unaware. I knew I had plenty. I just didn't see my plenty as any type of competition with God. The two were most certainly not connected because I was a good Christian woman doing good Christian things.

Meanwhile, my closet was packed to the brim and could sometimes be annoying. Hanger behind hanger. Clothes I had never worn and forgot I had, with tags still on them. Even with the few pounds I'd lost from being in Honduras and experiencing the unfortunate stomach incident, due to some soured *tres leches* cake, I was still a bit heavier than usual. And I was at a loss as to what to wear to an upcoming speaking event. My crowded closet wasn't making it easy on me.

So I called Shari.

Shari, the bubbly redhead, is one of my most favorite friends. She also happens to be a fashion stylist, which is convenient for times like this. Not used to inviting people into my closet, getting clothes advice, or making SOS calls, I trust Shari. Little did I know her coming was actually the date Jesus had marked on the calendar to put a stop to my lingering denial. Good thing I knew little, or I probably wouldn't have asked her to come. But Jesus does us the biggest favor when He puts a stop to things that are secretly chipping away at us. Tough love comes in different forms, and sometimes it looks more like the Sovereign ordaining someone to find out your secret than like your nonconfrontational best friend finally getting enough moxie to tell you some hard truth.

"Oh, my word—you have so many clothes, Lisa," Shari said, thumbing through my clothes with wide eyes and signature Shari laugh. "*I do?*" I asked, sincerely. I knew I had plenty. I just couldn't imagine a clothes person such as Shari thinking it was a lot. And that was *the moment*. Shari meant and thought nothing of her passing comment. She wasn't there to judge, nor is she the type. She was already back into her great outfit search, chatty and unaware, but my mind had now escaped us. I could see nothing but gross excess. Clothes I didn't wear. Clothes I couldn't fit into. Clothes, clothes, clothes, and shoes and hats and bags too. At some point I'd bought them all, probably for a bargain. And I'd probably felt proud.

I'm not proud now. I'm embarrassed.

For months, God had been readying my heart for Shari's passing comment to be my moment of cataclysmic conviction.

It was not about the amount of money I spent on clothes or items for my home. It wasn't about if I technically could afford them or if I bought things without going into debt. It was about what I had chosen over God sometimes to numb myself or give myself a high when I was sad or happy or bored. It was about what had become for me a "deadly over"—*over*indulging my visual wants and cravings and grossly making my life more complicated as a result. My having so many clothes that I didn't even know what to wear was the small symptom, but the big symptom was the angst, that nagging feeling of being out of control, which led to the cycle of guilt, regret, and justification when shopping. If I'd been honest with myself in so many of the moments I'd hid behind my swiped debit card, Jesus could have helped me. It was in *that* moment, in my closet with Shari, that I realized how I'd been putting myself over Jesus, even with the silly shopping I usually thought nothing of.

> If I'd been honest with myself in so many of the moments I'd hid behind my swiped debit card, Jesus could have helped me.

Three months after Shari visited me in my closet, I started my one-year shopping fast.

I did it for one whole year—buying nothing for myself that was a want versus a need in the clothes or home décor department (my two areas of historical overindulgence). I made it without buying a single thing, though at times I came close. I learned the art of having things in a cart, walking away, and not feeling embarrassed over it (sorry, all the store workers who found my abandoned carts). I got used to staying away from stores, completely. Over time, it became a new lifestyle. I felt God becoming more important to me than my momentary need to fix myself with something that will never fix me.

Maybe this comes easy for you—putting Jesus above yourself. But not over here. It's never easy for me to put Jesus over me. It's intense and upheaving and gets a tiny bit gnarly, and I don't normally use that word. If I look back in my life, I can see how nearly every decision to clear my life of the clutter it had accumulated (and, as a result, had started causing me pain in some way) grew into Jesus becoming more important, not less.

I wish our motives as humans were driven by sheer purity, but that's not how it typically goes. Discomfort is more likely our change agent, and I'm grateful Jesus accepts our meager starts, isn't snobby about our growth processes, and sticks around as we grow into rightly placed passion for Him.

Occasionally people have said to me, "I wish I were as strong as you," and I always want to either cry or laugh and say, "Are you kidding me? I've spent half my life feeling weak and internally terrified."

> I'm grateful Jesus accepts our meager starts, isn't snobby about our growth processes, and sticks around as we grow into rightly placed passion for Him.

Please don't think me some kind of spiritual freak. Most of the change God has done in me has come from me doing things the hard way, that is, *my way*. This is the upheaving of self, long buried in the denial tactics we humans are so good at mastering. Moments when I found myself in such a mess, with Jesus holding me as He cleaned my wounds, reminding me of His wellness plan. This is the gnarly priority reordering I previously mentioned, and I suspect you've been there too. I haven't forgotten that history. When you've been maimed from self-inflicted wounds, you don't soon forget. The truth is, I can't choose my way over Jesus' way anymore because I can't afford the scars. A Jesus-over-everything lifestyle is a *Jesus-take-over-me-and-my-lifestyle* so I don't ruin my one precious life. But even more than that, it's the understanding that the priority of Jesus brings order to the chaos of our lives, a job only God is big enough to do.

> A Jesus-over-everything lifestyle is the understanding that the priority of Jesus brings order to the chaos of our lives, a job only God is big enough to do.

If we want our lives to work, the Jesus-first life *is* the way. God doesn't want us to waste our lives trying to maneuver another way, making life more complicated in the process. As the Creator of the system of order, He knows how things will work. It is exactly as Jill Carattini, managing editor of *A Slice of Infinity* at Ravi Zacharias International Ministries, says,

There is a phrase in Latin that summarizes the idea that the shape of our deepest affections is the shape of our lives. *Lex orandi, lex credendi, lex vivendi* is an axiom of ancient Christianity, meaning: the rule of worship is the rule of belief is the rule of life. That is, our deepest affections (whatever it might be that we focus on most devotedly) shapes the way we believe and, in turn, the way we live. In a cultural ecosystem where we seem to worship possibilities, where freedom is understood as the absence of limitation upon our choices, and where the virtue of good multitasking has replaced the virtue of singleness of heart, it is understandable that we are both truly and metaphorically "all over the place"—mentally, spiritually, even bodily, in a state of perpetual possibility-seeking.[1]

Here's a piece of crucial news: it's not enough to go through life led by our cognition. It's not even enough to pray about things if we believe that releasing our burdens recuses us from next steps and we expect Jesus to do all the work from there. "If a person says to those who are cold and hungry, 'Go in peace; keep warm and well fed,' but does nothing about their physical needs, what good is it?" asks Yale theologian Miroslav Volf.[2] This is the reality of why many of us continue to experience being overwhelmed by our life, year after year. We beg God for help in the midst of a life with a mixed-up order of priorities and wonder why things aren't working; yet when we put Him over all the things on our list, myriad complications fall away. If you've ever done this, even in one decision, you know it's true. If you haven't yet, I hope you'll try it. We aren't pain-free, struggle-free, problem-free (John 16:33). But we have fewer complications, which is what is at the core of much of our daily angst.

I'm okay with it if you want to put Jesus over everything—starting with yourself—for a reason other than one that is superspiritual. Maybe you feel like it's the right thing to do. Maybe you feel it is expected of you as a follower of Jesus. Maybe your heart really isn't in it right now and you are leaning toward making the choice simply because you're embarrassed you never have before. Or maybe your decisions up to this point have created a complicated life or situation, and that's not the life you want, so it's more about finally trying it God's way. From someone who wildly reaped the benefits of a year's shopping fast—and who was largely embarrassed into it—let me just say that sometimes a bad reason to start is enough. And on this Jesus-over-everything journey, I have faith that if you stay committed to it, somewhere along the way it will become a new lifestyle.

And you'll want it this way because it is the way it's supposed to be.

WHAT'S NOT WORKING RIGHT NOW BUT CAN

Don't assume that because your life isn't working, you need a whole different life. Sometimes you need God to finally run yours. Too often we throw perfectly good lives in the trash in search of ones we end up tarnishing all over. The core of why our lives don't work isn't the life itself but what we internally never made right. This is why we wind up repeating patterns.

In the spirit of full disclosure, I should tell you that it wasn't the embarrassment alone that led me into the shopping fast, but also because on many levels, my closet wasn't working for me. With all the clothes behind clothes, so-much-in-my-closet-there-are-too-many-choices-it-is-frying-my-brain, it wasn't bringing me joy, and Marie Kondo wasn't around yet, telling us things like that. We innately know things that are not working for us. Sometimes we just don't know how to change.

> We innately know things that are not working for us. Sometimes we just don't know how to change.

I've watched humans awhile, and I have a theory. Despite our temporary feelings, there are three things that make our lives not work in the long term:

1. too many options
2. getting away with something that is not good for us
3. trying to handle everything ourselves

Too many options lead to mental confusion, second-guessing, and dissatisfaction with our lives. We spend our lives in angst over the great what ifs—what if we had picked that life or that spouse or that job or made that choice instead of this one, and the list goes on. We don't have to sit in scarcity, for the most part, and we are glad about that, but the allure of option is what actually drives us mad. More options are not what we are after. A less-complicated life is. Options will not help with that, but we like them, regardless.

Getting away with things we know aren't good for us isn't working for us either. For months, maybe years, I knew shopping wasn't holding me together. I knew it wasn't helping me live a more purposeful, focused life. It was muddying the waters. Many times I could have run to Jesus to help me sort out something, but I ran to Nordstrom Rack instead. Most of the time when I wanted something on sale, I really wanted His peace. I thwarted lasting spiritual thirst-quenching by taking water breaks. Every sinner grows weary enough eventually, and we want permanent deliverance—not just sips that get us by. It's a matter of how dehydrated we allow ourselves to become while on the journey. Admitting that something that isn't hurting us visibly is a sin is perhaps the hardest leap to make. Deflection is far easier, and a lot of us are experts.

And then there's the issue of our crippling belief in self-sufficiency. The most capable, independent human is one in whom perhaps God alone knows the weak spot. Eventually the bootstraps wear from over-pulling. The brute strength comes to an end. The flesh struggle never does. It's why promises of self-sufficiency are damaging to a world hungry to bypass God. We are eager for that message, though fools to believe it. If we could fast-track our process to getting what we want and go around God, we would, every time—He's too slow and generally uncooperative for our liking in most cases. We like our independence, and we may even do well with it for a time. But eventually we will let ourselves down and lose confidence in our abilities—a place where God can do some of His greatest work. And in that place we will desperately want someone to take care of us.

We like options until they make life too complicated.

We like doing what we want until our choices make matters worse.

We like our independence until we need to be taken care of.

Too often, when our lives no longer work, we assume it is time to get new lives: pull out of marriages, leave churches, search for quick fixes to solve money issues, cut friendships, move somewhere else, drop a project to start a new one. And at the end of the day, we are still left with

> Eventually we will let ourselves down and lose confidence in our abilities—a place where God can do some of His greatest work.

the hole within. What we actually need is for God to adjust the lives we have by taking over and running things. When we build a life on the priority of experiences, we can expect to get disillusioned by the highs and lows. Nothing is worse than living unsettled. Nothing is more symptomatic of human self-governance than living from high to high.

What is not working for you right now may look like shopping or any other excess or even something you don't see as excess. Giving up priority in your life to Jesus may not be your typical solution, but I can assure you, it's the key to making your life work.

WHY WE CAN'T BE FIRST

I do not do well with second place.

That tragic time in high school home ec, when we had a contest and I took home second place—the first-place-loser silver ribbon—after making an entire dress, was not a good day. My mom, being a master seamstress, already had me overblowing my abilities on a sewing machine, and I will testify firsthand that this is a skill not passed down through genetics. Forget that the dress wound up Barbie-sized, and I wasn't able to pull it up over my hips to see how it looked. In my mind it was a *Project Runway* dream. The winning title was practically stolen out from under me and given to the quiet girl in the corner who had been sewing since she was five. I don't know if that was her real story, but it's the one I told myself to cope with the loss.

As with most Jesus-over-everything realities we find much easier to read about than live, we may comprehend the priority order issue. But sometimes we just want to give our abilities a whirl. Some of us like the idea of control more than others (ahem), but we all like it, and because we are so easily enticed by our desires, it takes a pile of mess of our own doing to show us tangible proof of why us being boss doesn't work. Without the immeasurable gift of sovereignty, we are left with a serious case of being right in our own eyes—something I suspect we will die praying to overcome.

We can't be first because if we were,

we would make the wrong decision,
we would give someone bad advice,
we would quit before we should,
we would hang on to something we need to let go of and vice versa,
we wouldn't be able to keep the world spinning,
we wouldn't be able to prevent tragedies or pull off redemption, and
we couldn't save anyone from their sins.

These are just a few of the reasons we can't be first.

So then we are left to pray away this stubborn, misguided will that feeds us the ridiculous notion that we can do this thing better than God. We have skinned our knees so blessed many times, and we still think we won't fall down over this or that. Our decisions have been flighty and error filled, and we remain convinced we have the whole thing figured out. God holds none of this against us. But He'd like us to open our eyes and see. It is in our best interest that He is over everything, since He cannot make such mistakes.

Colossians 1:18 speaks beautifully about Jesus' positioning—the "preeminence" of Christ (KJV), which, in several translations, is substituted with *first place* (HCSB) or simply *first*. As Paul was writing to the church at Colossae, during his imprisonment in Rome, he was reminding people he had never met and only heard of that Jesus is enough. (This issue, the one we still struggle to grasp, is at the core of prioritization: do we believe He is *enough*?) These believers' reputation for mixing elements of paganism and secular philosophy with their Christian beliefs had reached Paul, and he was eager to give them a healthy dose of reality: "Look at all Jesus has done for you; remember who Jesus is; now make him number one" (vv. 12–23, author's paraphrase).

From Paul's words to our eyes, minds, and hearts today.

When we are tempted to take back authority in our lives, *Jesus first*.

When we forget how much we have made a mess running things, *Jesus first*.

When we start to think we might just want to take another crack at it and see how it goes, *Jesus first*.

Right now,

- look at all Jesus has done for you.
- remember who He is.
- decide if that is worth making Him number one.

DEADLY OVERS

I talk with people for a living, which is a humorous plot twist for an introvert who grew up hiding under tables at steak houses on Sunday afternoons after church so people wouldn't talk to me. Long before the *Jesus over Everything* podcast, I was traveling to places and speaking, meeting people at book tables and praying with them at altars, sandwiched between bleacher conversations with my kids' schoolmates' parents and coffee dates with friends and fellow life journeyers. I don't know how many people I've talked to in my life, but I do know this: we say many of the same things:

I apologize for everything.
I overbook myself because I don't want to let people down.
I get in my head and go down so many negative mental roads.
I constantly feel the need to explain myself.

We have the same look on our face with every confession: one of defeat, frustration, and pain. We long for that simpler life, where none of this is so complicated—people say what they mean, we take each other at face value, we don't feel such pressure to please or keep up, we leave room for mistakes, we don't feel used, and we stay committed at all costs. We have the same hopeful standards for ourselves, even if we see the gaps more clearly in others. We live in this land where over-*everything* rules, except Jesus isn't at the core of any of it or it wouldn't be so out of whack.

With sisterly love, I hope you'll let me clear this up. We do some of these things because we are under a false assumption of emotional martyrdom as if the overdoing is in some way producing the humility and selflessness we can't seem to otherwise find. But let me make this clear: these things are not spiritual. They are not a substitute for the Jesus-over-everything lifestyle that actually produces those spiritual character qualities required for maturity. If you keep reading, this book will give you the true picture. I'm asking you to stop settling for this other fake mess—the destructive *overs* we find ourselves too often picking, not even realizing how they've led our lives to become complicated—and to embrace instead the godly *overs* that make for a more fulfilled, thriving life. I think if

> We are under a false assumption of emotional martyrdom as if the overdoing is in some way producing the humility and selflessness we can't seem to otherwise find.

you'll give this a chance, you'll see your life turn into the more settled one you've wanted.

We've been living in a deadly land of overs for a while, many of us, trying to make life work by forcing empty, self-serving production. Putting Jesus first is choosing the better land, handing us back our sanity.

OVERDOING

I've had to face a lot of things about myself this year, and much of it hasn't been pretty.

I've found myself in a counselor's office for the first time in many years, and it's taken nearly an act of Congress to get me there. If I do second place poorly, I do weak and in need even worse. I trust slightly less than that. (Feel better about yourself? You're welcome.) The reasons it's taken me so long to get into the counselor's office have become some of the main topics we discuss during my visits. Blessed irony.

Even before I started seeing this counselor, as a psychology student for the better part of five years (four in college and one postgraduate), I've done a lot of my own homework. They say you should be through grieving after two years—whoever "they" are—but I say that's bull. You grieve forever when you lose someone you love; it just comes in waves. As life goes on, the waves come less often but are no less strong. Since my father died, I've been sorting through the regular grief, plus the extra layers of questioning my legacy and my DNA—figuring out who I am outside of him, which is no small feat since people want to make me into his clone. This week it's been some lighter revelations. I realize that I come from a long line of overdoers, particularly on my father's side, which brings up memories that make me smile.

My paternal grandmother, known in the days of ceramics for gifting nearly the entire world with some figurine from her very own kiln (I still have an angel she made somewhere around here), spent her latter days knitting every living president an afghan (I also have at least three afghans). Were she still alive, I feel confident she would show you the thank-you letters from them, with stamped signatures to prove it. My father, the proud driver of the largest truck man could own, with the largest tires to match, made quite an impression on the day he marched into my middle school with a yellow legal pad inscribed with three points (just like his sermons, the irony of which doesn't escape me) to lecture my PE teacher on why a C in her class was not acceptable for his little girl. A simple phone call for a man such as my father would never do. Both of these gems—Daddy and Grandma—are now in heaven, overdoing it somewhere together up there, I'm sure.

These are the fun memories, and then there are the harder ones too. Jesus wasn't at the forefront of my mind when I overindulged in sin or I wouldn't have done it. I've been like the Ephesians, forgetful of my first love (Revelation 2:4). The overdoing didn't start with my father's side of the family. It started further back than that—it's in the history and genetics of all of us—but it doesn't have to find comfortable residence with me unless I let it. Before Jesus can be over everything, we have to allow Him to remove from our lives what has thus far only complicated them.

OVERAPOLOGIZING

One of my most painful come-to-Jesus moments came about eight years ago through a volunteer assistant half my age. Sitting across the table from me at the cutest breakfast place in Franklin, Tennessee, Mary Kathryn said, "You apologize for your ministry, Lisa. Do you realize that?" I most certainly did not realize it, nor did I want this young woman I barely knew pointing it out.

"I do not," I told her flatly. I truly did not believe what she'd just said.

The older woman sitting with us, Shawna, piped in. "Yes, you do, Lisa. She's right."

I was having none of this, none of their harsh bluntness, none of these things they could not possibly know. I moved on to the next thing, red-faced and flustered, filing this moment away to analyze it by myself—or maybe not.

It took about five soul-searching years for me to finally face the reality: I *had* been apologizing for my ministry, among many other things, for years. Half my life had been spent apologizing for things I needed not apologize for—while, at the same time, holding back from the truly necessary "I'm sorrys"—because pride had fooled me into thinking my false humility was actually the real thing.

I apologized to my brother and sister for being the one who got the writing career, when both are better writers than me, by diminishing my writing accomplishments or not even talking about my new projects.

I apologized to that girlfriend I shared history with, who desperately wanted to be the next Beth Moore (her words) and started acting weird when she found out I was teaching the Bible, by downplaying my ministry anytime we talked about it over coffee so she wouldn't get upset.

I apologized to my friends whom I couldn't spend time with like I wanted because I was always working, feeling guilty every time we were together, thinking it wasn't enough.

> **Pride had fooled me into thinking my false humility was actually the real thing.**

I apologized for being successful to those who think I am and find me unworthy, and I apologized for being unsuccessful to those who invested time in me and I underperformed and disappointed them, and I apologized to those who think I shouldn't use words like *successful* about ministry at all.

I realized that in so many ways, my apologizing was not only unnecessary but also self-serving. It was not humble; it was humiliating. It lifted no one. It was not about God. It was about the emotional slums of humanity—me wanting to serve me, me wanting to get people to like me, me wanting to ease someone else's jealousy, me wanting to do work only God should do in all of us, the work only He can do.

And in the process I was watering down the beauty of true apology. I do not agree with people who tell us to hold back all the apologies. "I'm sorry" is a powerful practice—repentance and humility the result. Teri sent an Instagram DM to tell me as much:

> I've been in a season of overapologizing in so many aspects of my life, and it has dumbed down when I am truly sorry. In one aspect I apologize to someone I highly respect because I believe if I apologize for things they are irrationally upset about, they will approve or like me. In other ways I've been silently and verbally apologizing for my gifts. It has made me at times regret my calling because I don't feel accepted.

And so did Laura, who spoke about apology in this breathtaking way:

> My brother-in-law just died at the age of fifty-nine. By the end he was saying "I'm sorry," constantly, especially in my husband's presence. It was clear that he was in a state of deep repentance. Sometimes it takes that glimpse of eternity before we realize the value of repentance. It was hard to watch but so sweet to cover him with love and forgiveness.

I felt every word Laura wrote. My own father apologized like this in his final months as well, mostly to my mother, whom for years he had put through many difficult things without apology, as far as I know. It was belated, but it was still a gift. How sad it would have been had we all missed out on that piece of redemption had he bought the advice "Don't apologize." In my twenty-four-year marriage, had we bought into the idea from the iconic novel and subsequent movie *Love Story*, that "love means never having to say you're sorry," my husband

and I never would have stayed together. No one can offer the vulnerability and raw humanity a real marriage requires without our flaws inflicting pain on our partner at some point. Apologies are good vital signs in a healthy relationship.

Wisdom is not about never apologizing. It's about sincere apology when it's right.

OVEREXPLAINING

Six months ago I would have been convinced I do not have a problem with overexplaining. That is, until I introduced podcast interviews to my audience and started listening back to them in the editing stage, with a wince and one closed eye. In the first few months of interviews, the amount of time I took asking my guests questions, especially hard questions, was shocking. I found myself painfully restating things, when I'm sure the guests caught it the first time around. For the sake of the audience, so many of these moments didn't make it past the cutting-room floor. Nothing like listening to yourself on-air to no longer be able to deny your shortcomings. (Ever watched yourself on video? Listened back to a voicemail? Then you know exactly what I mean.)

A lot of us are chronic overexplainers. We feel our first stab at words wasn't good. What we are saying doesn't feel adequate. We may be trying to couch a hard truth that needs to be said, so we say it . . . and then say it again, and again, and maybe again, if we feel it necessary. My friend Tracy tells me she is learning that "it's okay to say no without giving all the reasons." That "no is a complete sentence." A big and hard-fought amen to that. Not everyone needs to know why you can't come to that dinner party—maybe your daughter has revealed to you something difficult, and you are not in a good place to go and pretend when your heart is in pain. It's okay not to go, and it's okay to say you aren't coming, but thank you, and leave it at that. And on that note, may we all be better accepters without demanding explanations.

Overexplaining is not simply being at a loss for good words, though I think it's what we feel at the time that drives us to put more words forward. It's about not feeling safe enough with each other to believe the other person won't fill in the gaps of a story he or she doesn't know. And it's about our need to control a narrative to ensure that doesn't happen. But what if we trusted God enough to help us heal from our micro-management of all that? What if we stopped stepping in and complicating things before He managed it in His time? The body of Christ needs Him in charge of our interactions to cover our silences and disappointments and bring understanding versus judgment—the way of unity. In that place, we can then trust that our lack of explaining will be met with understanding over the judgment we often feel.

OVERANALYZING

The world is full of thinkers and feelers, and both are a gift from God. Some of us come into this world with amazing natural radar. Add the Holy Spirit to that and you have a true gift to this world. Highly emotive people keep the rest of us accountable to the needs and hurts of folks—the world cannot exist without them. But thinking too much can also lead down dark roads. It can cause us to imagine things that aren't true, to make up entire narratives that hurt us unnecessarily. Relying on our feelings is dangerous as well. Feelings serve as a gauge but not a boss. As a creative, overanalyzing can cause me such pain because nothing is ever good enough—perfection creeps in, doubt takes over, and before I know it, I have become paralyzed by the thoughts in my head that don't have merit. This deadly "over" has taken up far too much time in my life through the years, and because we share humanity, I know I'm not alone.

OVERINDULGING

My shopping issues are a classic case of overindulging. But so are other things we like to ignore in a me-over-Jesus life. Eating. TV.

Drinking. Social media. Putting too much on our calendars. The danger is *we're numb to this list*. We've stopped being shocked by it, along with a lot of other things. Overindulgence is so common it doesn't seem like that big of a problem. Accountability seems antiquated and silly. Even little old ladies have their faces buried in a phone at the doctor's office now, so how can something that everyone does truly be harmful?

But get in a roomful of friends talking about everyday struggles, and phone addiction is one of the first things that will come up. We will talk about it more in a later chapter, but if you don't think we all aren't aware of how bound to our phones we've become, you're wrong. We are all talking about it. We just aren't doing much more than that.

The deadly over of overindulging has led to such problems for us—when self mandates standard, the limit is the sky, and the sky is too high. We aren't good at self-regulation. We choose the wrong things and try to make them right. Read Ecclesiastes. Solomon knew because he had tested the theory. Giving in to our temporary wants in light of the treasures of heaven isn't worth it. What we've gotten, most of the time, in return for our liberties is wild dissatisfaction and pain.

OVERWORKING

Several months ago I read a statement online attributed to author and Bible teacher Priscilla Shirer, and it stopped me in my tracks: "Overwork is unbelief."[3] It might, at first, be hard for us to make that mind-set leap—shrugging off the lighthearted suggestion from others that we are a workaholic or seeing our online hobby grow into a business we never intended to start—to the thought that our overworking is, in fact, not fully trusting in the promises of God. But would we be overworking if we felt like we were enough, just for who we were—if not to prove something to someone, escape from something, or acquire more out of a desire to gratify self? I know the argument. I could use it myself: *I just love to work*. And it's true. I do. I've worked since the minute I turned sixteen and Fishel Swimming Pool Center in Springfield, Missouri, was willing to hire me to test the pH levels in people's pool water. Achievement, creating, and progress all feel good to me, and the work I do now, I believe, is more important, focused, and God-ordained than ever.

But in the face of God asking me to cut some things out of my schedule and my subsequent fear that my lesser work production could result in disappointment to other people, He prompted this question: *Do you really want to be known as the woman who can produce?* I know well from working with leaders that burnout is sneaky; it comes on slowly but shuts things down immediately. We can see much clearer a God-ask to subtract negative things from our lives, but God's protection is often in asking us to cut out good things we don't see silently causing damage. As I considered God's question, I had to face the fact that at the core I was putting my work over trust and belief in Him. And I had to decide. As much as I love to work, I don't want to be known as the woman who can produce. That's an empty tagline with an expiration date of how long I'll be able to do so. I want to be known as a woman who follows Jesus, no matter what. In that tagline is a promise of longevity. Better for you and me to disappoint people than overwork ourselves into unwellness, as we've been at times apt to do. We would all do better to focus on the real work of becoming more like Christ and let Him birth and facilitate (and manage) healthy workflow from there. Sanctification over production every single day of the week.

I could list a bunch of statistics to prove to you we work too much, but we already know. We know because we have carpal tunnel from typing. We know because of the sales volume of those anti-strain glasses that protect our eyes from all the time we put in looking at computer screens. We know because we've been too busy with work to hang out with our kids, and now they're older and too busy for us. We know because we haven't had a decent vacation in years. We know because our overworked minds don't allow us a good night's rest.

Work is a precious, good thing, and we've often abused it. I'm not sure we even know how to do it balanced anymore because it's become such a part of our culture to burn the candle at both ends. I asked my friend Alli not long ago if there was a way to know if you work too much because, as you already know from reading, I struggle with that myself. Hard workers can become workaholics, content creators can become discontented, and influencers can become influenced by the need to produce before we know it, so Alli's wisdom was important: "When it becomes about you trying to earn worth through your work, you know it's gone too far." She added, "When the people around you that love you start telling you it's too much, it's too much." Such simple but solid and powerful litmus tests to go by.

I don't know what deadly overs are threatening to derail your Jesus-first life, but if you look at the root of your life complications, you'll find the answer. What's at the core of the issues you spend the most time cleaning up? Is it because of your overapologizing or overexplaining? Are your messes due to your overindulgences or over-working? Are you overanalyzing your situation, and your mind is a mess? I propose this with deep understanding: Jesus wasn't over everything in your life, or it wouldn't have been so.

LONGING FOR HOME

I never got the simple life I wanted.

I've been thinking about it a lot, thinking back to the simpler days when I was six. I didn't know much then about real life—about the highs and lows, the successes and failures. I just knew how to play. And cuddle kittens. And dream. And love Jesus. As much as I wish I could go back to that place where I didn't know about real life, I can't. And if I had, I would have missed out on the journey, so I don't truly want to.

What I want now is to have a beautiful, meaningful life that feels full and free. For Jesus to use me. I want the same things you want. Peace. Good food. Laughter. To feel loved and known and cared for. And there's something else. Even though I have a beautiful house and a family to spend my days with, I still live with a somewhat curious hunger for home. My friend and author Lore Wilbert said it best:

> We are born homesick, every one of us. We who live in this fractured world have eternity written on our hearts; we are longing to be home and are digging the tent pegs of our lives in as deep as we can get them until we arrive on eternity's shores.[4]

It's true. No matter how good a life we have, we will always long for our real home. It makes sense. We will never be satisfied here because this is not the home God made us for.

It is no wonder, then, that we struggle to live with the realities of our situation on earth: a complicated life made more complicated by the choices we make, often ruled by the flesh we want so desperately to die to. Bless us. It is a situation we all are in.

But it is not a situation without hope. God doesn't work that way.

In this life, the life where there will be trouble, there is also choice. The next eight chapters are dedicated to daily choices that support our Jesus-over-everything lifestyle, and my prayer is that with God's help you will find them more relatable, doable, and even delightful than you may think. There's nothing you can't do with Jesus. Now's a chance for you to put that belief into action.

To do this, you'll need to see your deadly overs (that is, *you* over Jesus) and Jesus-over-everything as two opposing lifestyles, and you'll have to decide which one you want. The way of life (aka the land of the deadly overs) that puts you in charge is guaranteed to stay complicated. You will keep overdoing it, keep picking the wrong over, and will have to live with the repercussions. I won't lie; it will often be the easier choice in the moment. And it's possibly the one you're most used to (I speak from experience). But it will have hidden problems, and it won't bring you the simplicity of good things you truly want in the end.

On the other hand, the Jesus-over-everything lifestyle (visualize this as the beautiful, fruitful opposing land) comes with a different kind of guarantee. If you choose to put Jesus in His place of pre-eminence, He will bless your life. He will sort out things that you've never been able to sort out before. He will do a perfect job at managing the imperfect life you haven't been capable of managing on your own. If that sounds good to you, I would just ask you to dive in and read this book to the end for the full picture.

Let's choose the Jesus-over-everything life, together, and as we do, imperfect as it will be, I'm praying that the Lord will guide us. I'm asking Him to point out the pitfalls and awaken us to the scorpions waiting to sting and help us keep our eyes on the land where we've chosen to live, never looking at the other land we think is better because Satan, in that moment, is using some kind of filter to brighten up those weeds.

I know that, right now, the thought of Jesus over everything may seem overwhelming or simply aspirational. What does that even look like? How is it possible in our day-to-day and practical situations? If Jesus is our everything, we have to put Him over all things, and we have plenty of opportunities to live out that kind of life daily. We've already determined that living in the land of the deadly overs has made our lives more complicated than it needs to be, so don't mentally complicate the Jesus-over-everything lifestyle right off the bat. It's actually quite simple. Life is about choice, and you're already making choices, every day. You just may just need to make some different ones. Every chapter we dive into from now until the end of the book will be daily lifestyle choices that either support the Jesus-over-everything lifestyle or move us away from it, and they are plain and simple. Real over pretty. Love over judgment. Holiness over freedom. Service over spotlight. Steady over hype. Wisdom over knowledge. Honesty over hiding. Commitment over mood.

In every chapter we will break these ideas down practically, to see what they can look like in our everyday life. We will talk about these things to help us see what the Jesus-over-everything decision is, how a Jesus-over-everything life is well within our ability to live, with the help of the Holy Spirit, and I will point you to some Scripture to help along the way. Jesus wouldn't have told us to put Him first if He wasn't willing to help us with the execution. The good news I'm telling you is this: you can absolutely live this kind of life.

And in all of this, I'm reminded of the famous verse, Joshua 24:15: "Choose today whom you will serve," and Joshua's own determination: "As for me and my house, we will serve the LORD" (ESV). You may have seen this verse seven hundred times on a laser-cut wooden sign and eight thousand times in a fancy font on a coffee mug, but don't miss the bigger meaning. Joshua wasn't making a statement for the back of a marriage ceremony bulletin. He was using his leadership to plead with a promise-breaking group of Israelites to do something new and radical for a change: to take their spiritual lives in a new direction. He was recapping God's goodness, just as Moses had done (in the book of Deuteronomy) before him. He was reminding them of the only way their lives would work from that point forward even as they lived in the blessed promised land.

Through Joshua, God was pointing out that even after all he had done, they had still chosen the other, less livable land. "With your very own eyes you saw what I did. Then you lived in the wilderness for many years" (v. 7). If I could offer my pedestrian paraphrase for the sake of the context of our conversation, it would be this: "You put Me over everything and saw how well that worked, and then you went back to that other land and put yourself back over Me, and it all fell to pieces."

And in a place of choice, once again, God asked them which land looked better and where they wanted to be.

Having experienced life in both lands, they knew.

"But the people answered Joshua, saying, 'We are determined to serve the LORD'" (v. 21).[5]

And with that, Joshua tells them the way.

"'All right then,' Joshua said, 'destroy the idols among you, and turn your hearts to the LORD, the God of Israel'" (v. 23).

It is where we, too, begin.

TWO

REAL OVER PRETTY

THEIR JOY WILL BE IN DOING WHAT'S
RIGHT AND BEING THEMSELVES, AND
NOT IN BEING AFFIRMED BY OTHERS.
—GALATIANS 6:4 TPT

I never met Luke Lang. But his words have consumed my thoughts for the better part of the day.

His last post on Facebook was on April 17, 2019.[1]

> We are home!!
> We were released from the hospital this afternoon. The doctor decided we couldn't do anything in the hospital that we couldn't do at our house, and the food is better. We didn't argue. It's good to be home.
> My oncologist and the team from Duke have put together a plan for my next step.
> We start a new chemo treatment Monday with some aggressive drugs that will require constant hydration.
> The secret weapon is a drug used for extreme lymphoma

and leukemia. I will bring home a lovely infusion pump so drugs will be pumping into me 24 hours a day. There is the possibility of some pretty dangerous side effects.

This HAS to work in order for us to go to Duke.

This is the last resort . . . that's the report.

We have cried a lot today.

We have cried out a lot.

We are crying out for a miracle.

We are crying out for resurrection.

It's time.

We want something to happen that no human can do.

That would be cool.

Five days later, Facebook reported, Luke died. Two hours and six months' worth of posts after I stumbled onto the whole situation, I emerged, wet-eyed and wishing I had met this man.

I was drawn to his wit in the face of the cancer dragon.

I was drawn to his real in the midst of social-media hair ads and smiling selfies and pictures of vacations we all save up a year for that never last long enough.

That day, especially, I'd seen all that enough. I didn't feel like riding the Christian inspiration wave, didn't feel like hearing an attagirl, didn't feel like a lecture in some Instagram post about how butter and cheese are going to kill me. I craved more of Luke's real even though he was now gone, so I went back in the archives: April 5, 2019.

AHOY and OWWIEE!

ARGHH!

This week has kicked me in the face, and gut, and pretty much every other body part.

I was given some NASTY new chemo drugs this week. I was warned.

I was told that the seas were about to get rocky.

I've been really weak.

The steroids have made my face look like a redfish.

My brain is as foggy as a murky old spyglass.

I've had a lot of fluids this week . . . I mean A LOT!

We discovered yesterday that I've retained twelve pounds of fluids.

I was sloshing when I walked and I was starting to look like the stay puft marshmellow [*sic*] man.

I'm now on a magic pill that causes me to go to the bathroom every eight minutes.

My legs have been very wobbly. I mentioned that earlier this week, I've had some very near and dear Pirate partners . . . to help me navigate my wobbly course. [They sent me] a very sweet walking stick. I'm not surprised, they are among many of the epic crew that have helped keep things steady during this journey. I'm so grateful.

Now sorry, but I've got to go pee AGAIN!

Post after post like that for months since his diagnosis. Some serious and poignant. Some dripping with sarcasm and talking about his new realities with nausea and pureed food. Most talking about Jesus. All of them fiercely real.

There is something refreshing about a person who shows us the real side of life, even if it's oversharing about his need to pee.

In this community of real we feel less alone. It is what all of us long to feel.

The good, the bad, the ugly, the complicated feelings, and all the mess that goes through our heads as we sort through it make us feel understood in our humanity. Some people keep things to themselves, and that doesn't make them any less real, maybe just more private.

But sharing the real stuff is a gift we offer to each other because it is something we need and crave. So it wouldn't be bad to push ourselves a bit.

In today's culture our internal personal battles are over whether to pretty up our real. Self-preservation is constantly on the forefront of our minds. Will we be acceptable just as we are? Or do we need a cleaned-up version for people to love us? Our real is offensive, even to us at times, and we are well aware that it could run some people off. It has before. We've been left alone after showing people who we are. It might not have had a thing to do with us. But we assume the correlation and silently vow never to show all our cards again.

But real is what makes us live without a facade or the complication of having to wonder if people accept the true us. Real is what changes people. It is what makes them decide they are willing to give Jesus a try. Real is what makes a story preach us a lifestyle sermon that sticks. Real heals us on a day that everything seems too perfect for us to fit in.

Real is what made me wish I'd known Luke.

JESUS WASN'T PRETTY

I didn't know until I was older that Jesus wasn't a mirror image of that tall, dark, and handsome man with the well-groomed facial hair who hung on our family room wall in a gold-framed picture for years when I was growing up. It's a picture my mind grapples with even today—the idea that He likely wasn't good-looking enough to be TV's next bachelor.

The Bible doesn't tell us exactly what Jesus looked like when He walked this earth, but scholars have done their best to piece it together. Scripture we do have that supports His everyday-man look ("he had no form or majesty that we should look at him, and no beauty that we should desire him," Isaiah 53:2 ESV) helps us conclude He wasn't the world's standard of physically attractive. It's hard for us not to imagine the tall, good-looking Jesus walking around, with people swooning at the mere sight. But it's not the case. Based on skeletal remains of first-century Jews, archaeologists have deduced that the average build of a male during the time of Jesus' public ministry was five foot one, 110 pounds. I hate to break the news if you didn't already realize it: Jesus wasn't pretty.[2]

Not in the worldly sense, that is, based on good looks.

Everything about His coming to earth was purposeful and specific, so this, too, must have been part of God's sovereign plan.

Perhaps if He had been attractive, we would make this the reason He drew so many people to Him or use it to explain the dedication of His followers. Perhaps then we would have felt as if He had a leg up on us regular people, who have flaws, things we believe require a filter, and it would have distanced us from Him.

Jesus drew people in because He was real, and that is the real attractiveness. Our true appeal will always be our truth lived out. To live a Jesus-over-everything life, we go to the core of why we follow Him to begin with: who He is, what He stood for, what drives His heart. While He walked this earth, He never tried to be anyone He wasn't. He never changed His truth to fit in. The strategy of heaven in God coming to earth in the form of His Son was not to gain popularity but to save souls from themselves. The cross wasn't pretty. It was brutal, humbling, and holy. It was real. What it does to change us, still today, is just as real.

> Jesus drew people in because He was real, and that is the real attractiveness. Our true appeal will always be our truth lived out.

We don't need to make ourselves look any better or keep up with some standard of attractiveness the world sets. This is the cause of so much of our wounding. My fashion consultant speaker/friend you read about in chapter 1, Shari, calls these *beauty wounds*, and I can think of plenty of mine, self-inflicted and otherwise. Trying to be skinny all my life has about killed me. Wishing I had fuller lips and prettier legs is something on which I've spent too much mental energy. Comments made by high school boys that I've never forgotten—even another woman who was supposed to be my friend but made a point to let me know we couldn't share clothes because she was smaller—these are marks that bore deep below the skin and stayed.

What we all need is to change our definition of what is truly worthy and attractive—being who we are and who we were meant to be, flaws and all. This evergreen message of identity is one we will always preach because humans will forever need it. But it's time to grow out of our obsession with ourselves and pursue identity with God, who created us, who cannot contradict His very nature to be exactly who He is. Self-focus has broken us in our reluctance to lift our gaze.

Jesus may not have been physically beautiful, but there is none more beautiful we could ever know. In His example we find our own guidebook for the attractive life we seek.

- He had beautiful strength.
  - He was tempted and didn't give in to it: "For we do not have a High Priest who cannot sympathize with our weaknesses, but was in all points tempted as we are, yet without sin" (Hebrews 4:15 NKJV).
- He had beautiful self-control.
  - He denied himself in order to do what God wanted: "Father, if it is Your will, take this cup away from Me; nevertheless not My will, but Yours, be done" (Luke 22:42 NKJV).
- He had a beautiful witness.
  - He developed a respectable reputation: "And Jesus increased in wisdom and stature, and in favor with God and man" (Luke 2:52 NKJV).

- He was beautifully gracious.
  - He was humble:

    Let this mind be in you which was also in Christ Jesus, who, being in the form of God, did not consider it robbery to be equal with God, but made Himself of no reputation, taking the form of a bondservant, and coming in the likeness of men. And being found in appearance as a man, He humbled Himself and became obedient to the point of death, even the death of the cross. (Philippians 2:5–8 NKJV)

- He was beautifully bold.
  - He took His appointment seriously and spoke the truth:

    For there is one God and one Mediator between God and men, the Man Christ Jesus, who gave Himself a ransom for all, to be testified in due time, for which I was appointed a preacher and an apostle—I am speaking the truth in Christ and not lying—a teacher of the Gentiles in faith and truth. (1 Timothy 2:5–7 NKJV)

- He was beautifully honest.
  - He cried and was real before God:

    Who, in the days of His flesh, when He had offered up prayers and supplications, with vehement cries and tears to Him who was able to save Him from death, and was heard because of His godly fear, though He was a Son, yet He learned obedience by the things which He suffered. (Hebrews 5:7–8 NKJV)

- He was a beautiful leader.
  - He was the ultimate example and went first:

    This hope we have as an anchor of the soul, both sure and steadfast, and which enters the Presence behind the veil, where the forerunner has entered for us, even Jesus, having become

High Priest forever according to the order of Melchizedek. (Hebrews 6:19–20 NKJV)

- He was beautifully empathetic and kind.
  - He could have pulled rank, but he didn't:
    Inasmuch then as the children have partaken of flesh and blood, He Himself likewise shared in the same, that through death He might destroy him who had the power of death, that is, the devil, and release those who through fear of death were all their lifetime subject to bondage. For indeed He does not give aid to angels, but He does give aid to the seed of Abraham. Therefore, in all things He had to be made like His brethren, that He might be a merciful and faithful High Priest in things pertaining to God, to make propitiation for the sins of the people. For in that He Himself has suffered, being tempted, He is able to aid those who are tempted. (Hebrews 2:14–17 NKJV)

All of these beautiful, true things about Jesus are what make Him real. They are what make Him trustworthy and worth following. They are why Jesus deserves to be first in the priority order of things and why being real is so important for us, that we would follow in the footsteps of the greatest role model we will ever know. We won't ever measure up to Jesus. But we are called to walk in His example. And that means choosing not to be pretty and dress ourselves up but to come real.

For to this you were called, because Christ also suffered for us, leaving us an example, that you should follow His steps:

"Who committed no sin,
Nor was deceit found in His mouth";

35

who, when He was reviled, did not revile in return; when He suffered, He did not threaten, but committed Himself to Him who judges righteously; who Himself bore our sins in His own body on the tree, that we, having died to sins, might live for righteousness—by whose stripes you were healed. (1 Peter 2:21–24 NKJV)

CHOOSE REAL

Right now the front shrubs that hug the front steps of my house like brackets look like my eyebrows: uneven. I'm more than a little embarrassed by both.

I'll get around to trimming the shrubs, but the eyebrows are a bit more of a sensitive subject than you might think. I never realized it until some professional head shots came back and to my horror, my eyebrows appeared to be in different time zones. At my age, it is not nearly as much fun as it used to be to take promotional pictures—the creases, lines, and spots are harder to hide. I don't want my picture taken. I can live with it, but only if my photographer is liberal with the editing.

After the initial shock and disappointment over a silly first-world-vanity/insecurity problem that is still humanly real, I spent some time with God. I know He will deal with me in the way He needs, not necessarily the way I want, and the first thing I have to come to grips with is that this is not about my stupid eyebrows.

It is about how I've been sucked into a societal mind-set that I must look as perfect as I can, so I am relevant in this beauty culture, where attractive people are rewarded with people listening to them. I've read the studies. I know that pretty people get further, have more clout, and, in this social media age, attract far more followers. It's hard not to get sucked into this social media bias nonsense that does exist.

I'll tell you something else real. The morning I had my picture taken was a hard one for me, and it showed on my face. I had heard bad news from home and had dealt with, perhaps, my most difficult parenting issue in twenty-one years. After two hours of sleep the night before, I woke up in a hotel room in another city and did the best I could to get ready for three back-to-back speaking sessions—and a photo shoot—with the lighting in a Fairfield Inn. My makeup fell short of covering the real me—the hurting me.

Looking at these pictures now, I admit that the crooked eyebrows are a silly nothing reminding me that, try as I may and pretty as I attempt to be, fake doesn't work. It's always going to be a no-go on perfection. None of us escape life without flaw. Behind every smiling moment, there are things happening that only God knows about and weeps over, and the pressure we put on ourselves to be amazing in the midst too often stifles necessary personal lament. I spent the whole blessed photo shoot with a cry-lump in my throat but a fantastic smile—and only one of those things was real.

I'm not saying we shouldn't sometimes hold it together. Sometimes, for a time, we have to. I'm saying to let those few-and-far-between moments remind us that at the end of the day, real may not be pretty, but it beautifully saves our hearts.

I wish someone had told me when I was a young woman that I could be real with the way I felt about my body and learn to love the size it was instead of trying so many damaging ways to keep it impossibly small.

I wish someone had told me I could be real about how hurt I was over church people gossiping about my family when my dad lost his church and was all over the news, instead of my developing a hard shell to make me tough so I didn't have to feel things.

I wish someone had told me I could be the real, feisty me and that it was good, not bad or too much for people to handle because that's what I believed all those years, despite my mother's love and approval (thankful for a good one), constantly trying to stifle a personality God gave me. When I was growing up, the church I knew wasn't as open as it is today to assertively gifted women.

Most of all I wish I had understood what scholar N. T. Wright said: "The authenticity that really matters is living in accordance with the genuine human being God is calling you to become."[3] I didn't know how to be me because I misunderstood the process of *becoming*. Too often the unfinished us is blind to what the Spirit-shaped us can be over time. Lies have felt true, damning, and permanent. We aren't weak for falling for them. We are human. But we need to put the truth of Jesus over them now.

I don't want you to go on believing any untrue things, like I have, so let me say it to you: real is the best pretty because it doesn't ask you to lie. Besides the fact that Jesus created us to be the real us, things get complicated when we try to live our life making it all look pretty; it's exhausting and discouraging to the rest of us who need someone, like Luke, to be real—about how hard the cancer is—about how adoptions aren't all roses even though we adore those babies, about how sometimes we don't want to put a bow on the end of our doubt or lament.

> **Real is the best pretty because it doesn't ask you to lie.**

It is hard as humans not to want to put our best faces forward, but it's far harder to spend a lifetime (or any amount of time) in pursuit of being loved and wanted for how we appear. I have lived long enough to learn this the hard way: if the goal in life is to be liked and accepted by everyone, welcome to a life of exhaustion. There might be nothing more detrimental to a soul (think: a deadly over) than daily overanalyzing how we appear to others and overworking to control it. Choosing real over pretty is choosing to free our souls from the grip of an overfocus on self—something that is the root cause of most of our distresses.

It also frees us to do what God created us to do—*be* who He created us to be, and this is our number-one lifework. Chasing pretty—curating a life appealing to everyone else—is at odds with why we are even here. I suspect this is why a lot of us stay wildly unfulfilled. We feel cornered into a contrived, half-baked, or even false persona we must keep up. What an exhausting way to live. It is the life of complication. Being real is a gift we give to others, yes, but it is also a gift we give ourselves. It releases us to be simple. We get to be who we are.

My daughter came home not long ago and told me a way her own version of this truth has released her, without knowing it was an experiment in real over pretty at all. It was the end of her sophomore year, and she was trying out for a coveted spot on the school media team, something she had looked forward to for years. It's a hard gig to land, and she was nervous. She had to make a video of herself talking, answering questions she didn't know in advance, and at the same time, skillfully acting natural. For a perfectionistic, hard-on-herself human, this was a combustible cocktail of not so easy to do.

"Be yourself," she whispered to herself before take 1, which came out in an unpolished, slightly clunky, but friendly and relaxed version of herself. *It's almost good enough*, she thought before trying again to make it better. Take 2 went off without a hitch, this version better than the first with respect to poise and word precision and overall performance. She was pleased and just about to delete the first version when a debate began inside her: *Do I put the more polished version of my submission forward, or do I submit the version where I am more myself?* Seconds later, quickly and before she could talk herself out of it, she hit delete on take 2—the polished take. She had decided that if she was to be chosen for the team, it would be because she was chosen for being *her*. As she told me this story, I smiled because I knew it was a precious good step on a lifelong road to self-acceptance victory for my girl—something many of us wish we had learned far earlier in life.

Staring down the fear that we won't be chosen if people know the real us is incredibly powerful. It is a precedent to start now, even if you're reading this at sixty-five years old and have never tried it before. The real us, who God made us to be—flaws, mistakes, bruises and all—is a mighty force for people to come to know Him. Choosing real is choosing Jesus because it's trusting His creative instincts that we were made good.

> **Choosing real is choosing Jesus because it's trusting His creative instincts that we were made good.**

Over and over again in the Word, Jesus speaks to us about how he chooses the real us. This from the One who knows the down and dirty. Let us not grow numb to stories like the one about the woman at the well, a woman who didn't have the right background and had dually not lived perfect—two big strikes for someone like Jesus to have anything to do with her. Quick to point out what to the Sovereign was already obvious, she said to Jesus, "You are a Jew, and I am a Samaritan woman. Why are you asking me for a drink?" (John 4:9). Jesus spoke into her real need and at the same time quenched *her* thirst—a thirst she didn't even know she had. Jesus answered, "Everyone who drinks this water will be thirsty again, but whoever drinks the water I give them will never thirst. Indeed, the water I give them will become in them a spring of water welling up to eternal life" (vv. 13–14 NIV).

We are all thirsty with the human need to be seen and validated, just like the woman at the well. Sometimes we know we are thirsty, but we can't pinpoint the exact place from which the thirst comes. Trial and error to quench the thirst is often met with dissatisfaction, but God is always dead-on. If Jesus had met us like He did the woman at the well, He would have encountered imperfect backgrounds and backstories and a lifetime of trying to figure out the best way not to let those things show. And we, too, would be refreshed by something far deeper than the physical water we drink, drinking in the endless supply of Jesus, who gives us the real thing: Himself.

The story of Zacchaeus, aka the wee little man from the tree (if you attended vacation Bible school as a kid), is another one not to gloss over. No one liked Zacchaeus—of that, his job as chief tax collector made sure. I'm taking liberties here, but I imagine him as annoyingly obnoxious—the one who butted in to lines, talked too loud, knew it all, and outdid every story—that guy no one wanted to be around. Maybe he hid his real behind his wealth and power. Maybe no one got to see his true self. Or maybe his real wasn't appealing to most people, and for the first time Someone gave him a chance, despite the fact that he wasn't all that great. What we know from the story is what happened after Jesus said he was going to Zacchaeus's house: something changed in the man's heart.

> Jesus entered Jericho and was passing through. A man was there by the name of Zacchaeus; he was a chief tax collector and was wealthy. He wanted to see who Jesus was, but because he was short he could not see over the crowd. So he ran ahead and climbed a sycamore-fig tree to see him, since Jesus was coming that way.
>
> When Jesus reached the spot, he looked up and said to him, "Zacchaeus, come down immediately. I must stay at your house today." So he came down at once and welcomed him gladly.
>
> All the people saw this and began to mutter, "He has gone to be the guest of a sinner."
>
> But Zacchaeus stood up and said to the Lord, "Look, Lord! Here and now I give half of my possessions to the poor, and if I have cheated anybody out of anything, I will pay back four times the amount."
>
> Jesus said to him, "Today salvation has come to this house, because this man, too, is a son of Abraham. For the Son of Man came to seek and to save the lost." (Luke 19:1–10 NIV)

This is what Jesus does so beautifully: He inspires us to rise to the people He created us to be by loving and accepting us just as we are. Name something more real than that. Where we are living below the potential He intends, He doesn't shame us into more; He motivates it. No one can get us to do the things Jesus can because no one has the power of conviction and the credibility in action that He holds. There's simply no equal by which we are moved to transform an entire way of thought or history. Only by Him, the Creator, Sustainer, and Savior of the universe, with His unmatched, proven track record.

> We may have hidden our real our whole lives, but one encounter with God and we can be inspired not only to be honest about who we are but also to change where we need to change.

Zacchaeus's response to Jesus was radical transformation. He became a man of generosity, benevolence, restoration, and humility simply because Jesus took an interest in him and became his friend. Never doubt the effect Jesus can have on your life or the life of another. We may have hidden our real our whole lives, but one encounter with God and we can be inspired not only to be honest about who we are but also to change where we need to change.

And finally let's look at the story told in John 8 about the woman caught in sin and about to be stoned, whose *real* was going to get her killed.

Jesus went to the Mount of Olives.

At dawn he appeared again in the temple courts, where all the people gathered around him, and he sat down to teach them. The teachers of the law and the Pharisees brought in a woman caught in adultery. They made her stand before the group and said to Jesus, "Teacher, this woman was caught in the act of adultery. In the Law Moses commanded us to stone such women. Now what do you say?" They were using this question as a trap, in order to have a basis for accusing him.

But Jesus bent down and started to write on the ground with his finger. When they kept on questioning him, he straightened up and said to them, "Let any one of you who is without sin be the first to throw a stone at her." Again he stooped down and wrote on the ground.

At this, those who heard began to go away one at a time, the older ones first, until only Jesus was left, with the woman still standing there. Jesus straightened up and asked her, "Woman, where are they? Has no one condemned you?"

"No one, sir," she said.

"Then neither do I condemn you," Jesus declared. "Go now and leave your life of sin." (vv. 1–11 NIV)

Time and again, He's saying to us through these and other stories: *I choose you, just as you are. You don't have to be pretty or pretend in front of Me. I already know.* Make no mistake: there's accountability in the John 8 story, just as in every story like it where Jesus heals, loves, accepts first, and then makes the path of holiness and next steps clear ("Go now and leave your life of sin," v. 11 NIV). There are bigger contextual pictures to this story, but the summation for us, as humans, remains the same: If God accepts our real self, there is no one left to matter. We don't get prettier before we come to God; we get more stripped down, humble, and repentant. One is born of performance. The other is born of truth.

And I know: sometimes we fear being real because we aren't in a place where we are representing Jesus well, and our real might be detrimental. With real lives on the line for eternity, that's something to get worked out, and Jesus will help with that, often in ways we don't prefer but that are necessary. Sometimes we have to get wrecked to get real. If you're there, don't despise it. God intends it for good, all the way around. Lift your chin. There's beauty to this. Often after a wrecking is a reckoning and a reuniting. Jesus is worth the loss of everything you know deep down isn't sustainable but hate to let go.

Let Him prove that to you even as that veneer you've spent your life creating breaks down before your eyes.

Whether it be in your life or in the life of someone else—watch the trend of crisis. It tells us what matters most. No one cares about anything pretty when something hard comes up. People innately know things will crumble under a glossy facade. The first thing to go in a moment of real trouble is social media, the thing in our daily life we think we can't live without: "I'm taking a break to deal with some things and work on myself." Because scrolling, online articles, and YouTube videos entertain us, but they don't help us sort out our lives. They're novocaine: temporary, but they don't heal deep places in our heart. Real conversations in small groups that dig junk out can do that. People sharing their raw and hard truths and, yes, sometimes even good old Facebook can produce that in a gem like Luke Lang, who will pop up in a scroll and take your breath away by his refusal to hide his raw and real.

About Luke. I would have stopped reading if he had tried to make cancer look prettier than it is. I walked through it closely enough with my dear friend Jennifer to get an education in its brutality, firsthand. Sugarcoating the real stuff that bonds us in our humanity robs us of community. I've watched what happens when twelve women are sitting around and I ask "what is the greatest need of your heart right now?" and a woman's guard comes down, and she uses words like "I'm scared" or "I feel forgotten;" then there's the gorgeous ripple effect of real that her words produce in others who feel safe enough to admit they feel the same.

May people get this gift from us.

Choosing pretty has led to insecurity and self-focus. Choosing real has led to freedom.

Choosing pretty has shown people a facade, with hollow result. Choosing real has impacted people's lives, sometimes for eternity.

Choosing real is living a Jesus-over-everything life.

LUKE LANG, FACEBOOK, MARCH 21, 2019: ─────────

Purée.

During my last hospital stay I got some fun, culinary news.

The Doctor put me on a purée diet for at least a month.

That means everything has to be soft, real soft.

Purée means to liquify solid food.

Everything I eat has to be creamy or pasty.

I can't have crunchy, which is sad because I love crunchy.

HELLO TACOS!!

There are some things that are naturally soft, things that I'm fond of like ice cream and gravy.

I've consumed a lot of pudding and yogurt.

I'm alright with all of that.

I've needed some help with the rest.

My amazing, super resourceful sister sent me some preassembled purée.

She found cans of mushy BBQ Beef and boxes of fun food items.

I get amazon boxes full of precooked kindness . . .

I save a ton of time at mealtime because I don't have to chew.

Here's something I've been chewing onto today . . .

I have realized that in the last several months God has puréed my heart.

He has softened my heart.

"I will give them one heart, and a new spirit I will put within them. I will remove the heart of stone from their flesh and give them a heart of flesh."—Ezekiel 11:19 [esv]

I have been exposed to a whole new world . . . a circle of suffering. My heart has softened as I have seen others hurt, walk with compassion, and cling to hope.

I have gotten to know my friend, the Holy Spirit, like never before. He walks with me, I hear His voice, I feel His tender touch. I have truly fallen in love with Him like never before. He gives me courage and creativity.

I'm different as the result of disease.

I cry a lot these days . . .

It's not because of the pain.

It's because my heart has been puréed.

Rest in peace, Luke.

Thanks for leaving us with your real.

THREE

LOVE OVER JUDGMENT

LOVE IS SAFE. LOVE IS STRONG[ER].
LOVE IS SUPER-SIZED.
—LUKE LANG

We love what makes us feel safe.

That is especially true during life's painful moments because pain has a way of exposing our greatest insecurities. We are desperate to find a shelter to feel protected from strong winds. Me? I love music. It was a source of comfort to me during my growing-up years; it made me feel safe from the blowing winds that encircled me:

> **We love what makes us feel safe.**

in Enid, Oklahoma, when, at age six, an older neighbor boy visited me in my tree fort one day and slid his hand up and down my hip curve over my patched jeans—which didn't feel right, but I never said anything

in Lake Jackson, Texas, whenever there was behind-the-scenes turmoil between Daddy and someone in the church that caused him to come home troubled

in San Jose, California, when Daddy wanted to leave another
church again, so soon, and I really loved that one

in Houston, Texas, when I suffered from mononucleosis for
months, and Mommy was getting strange prank calls that
scared me

in Springfield, Missouri, when Daddy got in trouble with the
IRS, and everything changed forever

All those times I had Evie and Amy Grant and the Imperials. And then I got older and snuck the other stuff in—Prince and Whitney Houston and Madonna and Bon Jovi. And Ratt too. I had my piano, which I played and played, often losing track of time. I sang and played from all the piano books Mom bought me—but my favorite was, of course, Amy. When I played her songs, I felt safe. I didn't worry about church problems. I didn't worry about moving again because I knew the music would go with me. The music would stay the same even when everything else was shifting.

I love Jesus for the same reason. At every stop on the map of my life, He has been the safe place for me.

My friend Brandi wrote something online not long ago that expressed in a few words what I've been trying to figure out for years. Writing about an extremely difficult time in her life from a few years earlier, she kept repeating the words, over and over, *I am safe with Jesus.* The words brought calm to her spirit. They made her open and tender when she wanted to close off. As soon as I read her words, I began to cry. The words are so simple, yet I've never needed to read anything more in my life.

I struggle to trust, even as an adult. But what I really struggle with is to feel safe. I've felt the judgment of the church when my father fell from his pastoral position but also before that. Kids have good ears, and I heard what people said when they thought I wasn't listening. I've felt judged for being too outspoken because girls should be quiet and calm, or at least that's what girls in the '70s and '80s in Christian culture were supposed to be. I don't know one person who hasn't felt judgment for one thing or another, often from inner voices, even before outside judgment comes.

If love often comes from a place of safety, then judgment often comes from a place of fear. Our easiest reaction to something we fear is to judge it because judgment allows us to quickly dismiss. (No one likes the emotion of fear, so our goal when we experience it is typically to release it as soon as possible.) It is why we so often turn to judgment, being the instant culture that we are, because it does not require of us the way love does. But it also doesn't reward us as love does.

Because we are often busy reacting to our fears instead of investing in love, we are constantly on the love search. In the long run judgment is empty. Even in the moments after we judge something or someone, it doesn't feel good or right—we may have dismissed the object of our judgment, but we can't dismiss the fallout to our own soul. It's become like a stain we tried to remove unsuccessfully out of the carpet, and now we are left to pass by it and remember. So please don't buy into this notion that the quicker way of judgment will make things less complicated for you. Mentally and emotionally, it just brings more baggage.

Love, though, uncomplicates nearly everything even though it's a more thoughtful and, yes, often time-consuming process. I read a tweet by comedian Wanda Sykes the other day that moved me so deeply: "Sobbing, missing my grandmother. Yeah, it's been 35 yrs, but, she loved me."[1] There were 85,700 likes and 2,980 retweets at the time I read it, and that doesn't count the responses back, so it moved a lot of other people too. We love those who help us feel safe and known and cared for.

All of this perfectly describes Jesus and why I can't quit the One I trust the most. There is no one safer than Jesus. No worry of betrayal, no worry He will turn His back and walk away. He's never told a thing I've told Him. He's never been absent when I needed Him most. We may never feel safe with anyone else, but we can always feel safe with Jesus.

If love often comes from a place of safety, then judgment often comes from a place of fear.

And, in turn, as we learn from Him, we will love people when we make them feel safe with us. This is why it is a better choice than judgment because judgment feels like pushing someone out into the cold, and Jesus is never about that. When people know that we are that corner to take refuge in from the storm—not the same refuge as Jesus but a safe human refuge in a world that feels disconnected and bitter—they will feel safe.

Safe doesn't mean *without conviction*. That is where we go so wrong. In *Put Your Warrior Boots On*, I wrote that love is in itself a conviction and that not judging people in no way means you water down a standard. The kind of safe love I'm talking about means *no matter who you are and what you've done, I will not reject you*. We don't have to wonder what Jesus would do. He would make people feel loved by making them feel *safe*. He did, all throughout Scripture. And in that place of comfort, we show people the character of God and lead them to the One who truly shelters and heals.

It is always the love that calms the most afraid, draws in the skeptics, brings back the prodigals, and changes the hardest hearts. Judgment can never do that.

WHY WE JUDGE

I won't spend even a paragraph of this book trying to convince you not to judge. If we don't understand why love is better than judgment, five thousand words won't convince us. That's a heart matter no writer can solve.

The better use of this conversation is to talk about *why* we turn to such a dead-end relationship option when we know, cognitively, it will never work and it complicates our lives by having us fulfill a role of

Discern vs Judged vs Condemned · *spirit of love*

decision-making that we are not capable of fulfilling. No one, including you or me, is ever *really* drawn to Jesus by experiencing judgment. Judgment is divisive, confusing, and unproductive, which makes it all the more curious why our flesh pulls us to it so many times. But here are the unveiled facts about judgment:

1. We judge when we're afraid.

   Ignorance and fear are the leading reasons we judge people—fear being at the very top. It drives our inability to love people like Jesus loves, and people feel it. We fear their sin will *rub off on us* as if by some sin transfer system that doesn't exist. We don't want their "leprosy," the very thing Jesus made a beeline to heal. We judge what we do not know, what we have not experienced, what we do not understand because we fear not being able to handle those realities. We don't want to associate with a tax collector even though we are tax collectors ourselves. Fear keeps us from being able to see people for who they really are and give them the benefit of the doubt for who they can become through the power of Jesus Christ.

2. We justify judgment with our Bible.

   This is the worst misuse of the Word, but I dare say we've all done it a time or two. The most dangerous person in the world is the one who is schooled in Scripture and slices people with it. The Bible sharply convicts as a sword, but it is never to be used as a weapon. In human hands with a human motive, it can be deadly and detrimental to the actual gospel. Even the most astute theologians do not agree on all things, and even as we use the Bible as our personal compass, we stay in accountability with Jesus as we run our individual races. Jesus is clear on judging in Matthew 7:1–5, yet even in that clear stance, only God knows the hearts and minds of people and where we personally fall. It's true that Jesus did say we can draw conclusions from the fruit we see (vv. 15–20), but putting ourselves in the judge's seat reserved for God is not a wise plan. He is fully capable of the job many of us try to do on a daily basis.

3. We justify judgment by making lump assessments.

We have some grand excuses for our prejudice when we feel justified in judging a group of people based on the behavior of someone who is *in that group*. A lot of us have stopped going to church because one person in the church deeply hurt us or a minister in the news behaved poorly, and now we judge all the leaders and churches the same. We have formed feelings and opinions about a person of another race because someone else of that race personally hurt us, hurt people we know and love, or publicly behaved badly.

Lumping everyone in a category instead of considering each person as she comes into our lives, finding out who she is and what her story is, and seeing who God made her to be is damaging and unfruitful. (One of my favorite things about God is how He died for the collective of us yet created us, loves us, knows us, gifted us, cares for us all, and saves us individually.)

If we want to lump people into any category, let it be lumping them into the category of people we deeply love. I heard recently that a church put the following statement on their sign outside, and it's such a powerful word: "Just love everyone. I will sort them all out later.—God." I can't give you a specific chapter and verse in the Bible that says that exactly, but I would suggest that the Word says that very thing throughout, loud and clear. I'm just grateful the sorting out isn't any of our roles down here. We'd all be in over our heads.

4. We judge because we recognize in others what we don't like in ourselves.

So often you can find us being the hardest on someone we see reflected in ourselves. We feel put off by the things we recognize as places we need to work on, sins we struggle with, characteristics we deeply wish away. It's easier for us to judge people than to deal with the fact that we are disappointed in ourselves or to work on getting better. The way we judge others for the things we recognize in us is a sign that we are struggling to love ourselves, first, which makes it impossible for us to love another.

A life of judgment never fulfills and results in feelings of loneliness and resentment. It may be easier to choose judgment, but it's healthier to choose love. C. S. Lewis said this:

> To love at all is to be vulnerable. Love anything, and your heart will certainly be wrung and possibly be broken. . . . Wrap it carefully round with hobbies and little luxuries; avoid all entanglements; lock it up safe in the casket or coffin of your selfishness. But in that casket—safe, dark, motionless, airless—it will change. It will not be broken; it will become unbreakable, impenetrable, irredeemable.[2]

Love is the gift that frees us from the death of never truly living. It helps us live lighter, kinder, wiser, fuller, not only to others but also to ourselves. Judgment is the easy go-to when we have shut ourselves off from love for too long. Jesus didn't stop at saying that judging others is an unspiritual way to live. He showed us with His own life how to choose the superior path of love. Judgment is a soul cancer—it attacks us from the inside and eats away at our ability to live strong lives. Love is the antidote for that.

LOVE IS STRONG[ER]

Love is safe, and love is also strong. It is as easy a choice and as disciplined as an ongoing matter of prayer to be able to live out.

I got a front-row seat to this truth being played out my whole life in my parents' relationship but especially in my father's latter years. Mom always took care of Dad. Though he was physically stronger with a bolder personality, on the inside he was intensely more fragile. Mom's calming spirit became necessary for life's many twists and turns, dark valleys, missteps, and a large IRS court case and subsequent judgment against Daddy that threatened to derail our family as its news was splashed all across town. Some of my most vivid childhood memories are of Mom picking up after Dad, plating his dinner, finding his lost wallet as he raced out the door. Never did she complain. Always did she take care of him.

My mother, a tiny woman, never lacked in determination. As much as she took care of my dad, she took care of everything else too—which no one knew would prove to be a necessary skill in the years to come, with Dad's failing health, when she would take on all the household responsibilities. Daddy ran the show, but Mom managed it. Without her, the furniture never would have been moved, rooms never would have gotten painted, and us kids never would have had a single warm meal or gone anywhere for fun. Mom did it all, for the most part. I never doubted that she was smart or capable. But because I was a different kind of female—strong-willed, determined, nontraditional in many ways, and too modern to wait hand and foot on any man—I wondered at times if she was truly strong. So we talked about it one day, in a rather heated discussion, in the bathroom. I asked her why she not only served my dad like she did but also stayed married to him when he had put her through so much all those years, not understanding in my youth how her decisions could be anything but weak and subservient.

"I made a choice," she said.

It was then, if for the first time, it dawned on me the why and how behind everything throughout my life, between my parents and who Mom really was at the core. She wasn't weak because she did those things I didn't always understand. She was strong because she made a choice—to love God and to love and serve my father as a result. The decision I saw lived out in front of me flowed from a bigger decision that was made first.

I knew something else about my mom as well, watching her all those years. Her loving my dad didn't end with a choice. Choice is where it started, but prayer was the continual next step to be able to pull it off, especially when things were the hardest. My mother was (and is) a woman of prayer. She had to be, to endure the deep valleys with my father. She had to be, to live out her choice to love him in the years he wasn't easy to love. It wasn't about having brute, willed strength. It was about having deep, inner strength that makes a choice to love and then supports it with an ongoing prayer life. There is no other way to live out that kind of love.

Let me just tell you what kind of love it turned out to be.

The last year of Dad's life, after multiple misdiagnoses and finally being correctly diagnosed with PSP (progressive supranuclear palsy)—a rare brain disorder doctors believe he may have contracted in the Navy working in the boiler room—when he could no longer walk, Mom would summon her stubborn will (seems I did get it honest) and God-given strength and implement unorthodox ways to maneuver my much bigger dad into a wheelchair and take him wherever he wanted and needed to go. It was never easy, but Mom loved dad, so she did it with joy. She carted him to doctor's visits, my kids' ball games, church, and to the storage shed, of all the crazy places. (I think it made Daddy feel normal somehow to riffle through old boxes of sermons and such.) She was his nurse in every sense that last year of his life, doing all the nursing things—things a couple never really intend to do when in their youth they become lifelong partners. Never was her strength more evident.

And then, finally, it was Dad's last day here. My husband, Scotty, and I had gone to my parents' home that beautiful Sunday morning of his passing. We gathered with Mom for prayer, and we all said good-bye, watched him leave earth, and then waited for the funeral home to take him away. The hospice nurse (my beautiful sister-in-law, Lynda) was standing nearby when I heard my mother ask, "May I change his socks?" An audible hush fell in what was otherwise a room buzzing with activity. The moment, undoubtedly holy. Mom added, before Lynda could say a word, "I've been changing his socks for almost a year now, and I'd like to do it one more time." Even in the end, never did she complain. Always did she take care of him.

We watched while my mother changed my father's socks for the very last time, witnessing her last choice to love someone she'd chosen to love over and over again. I've seen love be strong. I've seen it be stronger than anything else, even death.

Breathtaking.

We don't always make it easy for people to love us, yet we aren't exempt from it when someone makes it hard on us. Jesus modeled the choice to love without the loved party being deserving, a concept most disagreeable with our flesh. How do we possibly do this, you ask? First, I will tell you that *real* love is stronger than you think. My mom showed me that. Then I will tell you that it is a choice carried out by prayer, over and over again, for God to help us. I know the things my mother had to do to take care of my father in the last six months when she was his nurse. He was a mellowed and, in many ways, changed man, and Mom, a caretaker at heart, always called him "a precious patient." But on a core human level, the things she did would require prayer—no one is good enough or strong enough to care for such primal needs of another person. A choice to love would last only so long for any of us.

Love is stronger than fear, betrayal, anger, resentment, doubt, disappointment, and, yes, judgment because we chose God and God is love—the ultimate love. It's ours if we want it, choose it, and pray to live it, every day. When someone is unlovable and we love that person anyway, we are shadowing God. This is what being a Jesus follower means. We may think loving someone is about them. But, ultimately, it's about Him. Our behavior flows from there.

But it's not just that real love is strong, though that would be enough. It is that it is stronger. It is the 1 John 4:4 principle: "You, dear children, are from God and have overcome . . . because the one who is in you is greater than the one who is in the world" (NIV). Love has overcome many barriers nothing else ever could. Judgment separates. Love joins. The damage that judgment does, love can do

> We may think loving someone is about them. But, ultimately, it's about Him.

much to mend. It has the strength to pull people with grudges and long-held resentment back together. It dries up many tears. As Jesus showed us in the ultimate act of love on the cross, it is stronger than any act of man or evil.

LOVE IS STRONGER THAN HATE

Our city was changed forever when our beloved University of North Carolina at Charlotte experienced a school shooting on the last day of classes for the spring semester of 2018. Whenever something like this happens, we get a necessary wake-up call from the polarization of politics, and become, instead, humans bonded in grief. As a society we are all so weary of happenings like this—keenly aware of the pain and evil—and we long for answers. We may debate how to get there, but ultimately what we all want is the same: to find and exercise love rather than hate. We are exhausted by fighting, discouraged by cowardice, disillusioned by fear.

As believers, we can join a defeated bandwagon or rise and lead. Our Leader, Jesus Christ, set the example on the cross, with the response to any kind of hate: "This is how we know what love is: Jesus Christ laid down his life for us. And we ought to lay down our lives for our brothers and sisters" (1 John 3:16 NIV).

Rather than become so affected by the world's evil that we become ineffective, even as we mourn and grieve (which is itself a powerful and active part of loving people), we rise and lead in the way we say no to hate ourselves. We aren't Jesus, so the laying down of our lives would pale in comparison to the act of sacrifice on the cross, but we can sacrifice in our daily life. How? By standing against violence and racism (saying no to racist jokes and stereotypes). By defending widows and orphans in whatever way God leads (James 1:27). By refusing to allow gossip or division in our midst. By taking people in and by clothing and feeding them. Pray and use the imagination God gave you and think out of the box—the opportunities to "lay down our lives" for others are endless. If we are looking to love people, God will surely give us the chance.

It is really true what Dr. Martin Luther King Jr. once said: "Darkness cannot drive out darkness; only light can do that. Hate cannot drive out hate; only love can do that."[3] The sheer force of love is the only thing stronger than the vile hate that leads to things like racism and school shootings. Yes, let's educate. Yes, let's better understand and have more resources for mental health. And, yes, let's even advocate for stricter gun laws. But at the end of the day, let's do heart work and ask Jesus to help us love. It has the strength to overcome so much.

LOVE IS STRONGER THAN PASSIVITY

It's in our nature to self-preserve. But when we love like Jesus, when we choose the Jesus-over-everything life, we move past our own self-interest. It is not possible within our flesh, but with Him, it is.

In the middle of writing this book, I ran into my good friend Angela at a baby shower, and she asked how the writing process was going. I was honest and told her how it was challenging me and how I knew it was going to be challenging, too, for the body of Christ—how sometimes, even though I know God has called me to speak hard truth,

I can't lie and say I always love it. I've told God many times how much I wish He would give me lighter and more palatable things to share.

Angela, whose experience with her teenage son going to heaven I wrote about in *Put Your Warrior Boots On*, stared at me hard and said to me through tears, "I'm going to tell you this right now. Those lighter messages are nice sometimes, but they don't prepare me for walking this world when hard life hits. So keep sharing truth."

I know exactly what she means. The messages that have been my greatest travel companions have been some of the hardest to hear. I may have been resistant in the moment, but in the end I've concluded that the people who have been the messengers are the ones who have truly loved me enough to deliver the messages. So never measure your love by what your fear has convinced you to hold back, my friend. Measure your love by what your passion and courage have pressed you to love someone enough to say.

And, yes, there will be times that love has us saying nothing at all. Love can be silent—Jesus often was. That takes discipline, and it can still be strong, active love. In both cases there is this thread: love denies self-interest even if it costs us. Love is not being passive so we can gather likes and cheers. It is loving people enough to risk losing popularity. It is loving like Jesus, which means we risk misunderstanding and even judgment coming our way and learn to embrace it for the greater good of the gospel. We can be popular, or we can be His. Self-preservation is at odds with the Jesus-over-everything life. It is as my friend, author Sharon Hodde Miller said to me: when we want people to like us and thereby continue on in our passivity, we "set them up to continue on in error." (A request to my friends: please love me enough that you don't keep letting me make some bonehead mistake if you see that's the way I'm headed.)

This mind-set shift may also take a bit of retraining. Self-interest over love is a long-held reality for most of us. It won't die easily, so don't give up.

> **Love is not being passive so we can gather likes and cheers. It is loving people enough to risk losing popularity.**

Our lives are often complicated because of this very thing: we have spent time trying to get people to love us by largely staying out of their lives or compromising to a place of comfortable agreement. The gospel, on the other hand, promotes accountability and unified community. Uniformity isn't love. Unity comes through humility, not in morphing to all look and sound the same. Our goal, in many cases, has been the passive approach, and we have wound up in problematic relationships, often with friends taking us down in some way with them as they stumble and fall. Love can't tolerate watching people live unwell. The goal is their health and transformation and, in the process, our joy and fulfillment at having been a voice God used. But the relationship may be strained for a while, and we have to be willing to love people enough to sit in that tension and trust God.

There is nothing passive about true love. You run toward it, fight for it, do everything you can to hold on to it and nurture it so it doesn't leave. Resting and trusting God is also active, though our hands and feet may be inactive in the process. Song of Songs is a gorgeous picture of the intensity of love, and though it's on one hand about the love in a relationship between man and wife, it's an overall picture of how severe and concentrated true love is. Chapter 8 holds one of its many powerful word pictures: "Many waters cannot quench love; rivers cannot sweep it away" (v. 7 NIV).

Our world is full of passive bystanders to injustice and immorality—watching us wreck our lives as we go down dangerous moral and mental roads without someone to love us enough to help us by saying, "That's not the best place for you to be," or "That could affect your family, so why do it?" or "That's not who you really are, so don't waste your life playing around with something that will hurt you." We are so afraid not to offend; we don't want to say anything, and we don't know how to do it without bringing far more flesh than Jesus into it because (brace yourself for an ouch) we have a lazy relationship with the Holy Spirit. At the core of it all is self-interest. We often do not get involved, not because we care about honoring others' independence but because we care about preserving ourselves.

> Love can't tolerate watching people live unwell.

We wouldn't do that if someone were about to drive off an actual cliff. Good-hearted humanity wouldn't let us. Godly love then should be even stronger—strong enough to push past passivity and warn someone about that behavioral, emotional, or relational cliff she's headed straight toward.

LOVE IS STRONGER THAN SELF-LOATHING

Sometimes the biggest lessons in judgment are pointed at ourselves.

In this season of life I'm learning to treat myself kinder, and that has been a long time coming. My dad's CB handle was Pulpit Pounder—if you are old enough to even know what the term *CB handle* means (a CB was a citizens band two-way radio, used mostly by big truckers in the 1970s—the '70s version of Voxer), and that should tell you about the genes of my intensity. I came into this world being hard on myself for basically everything, and in many ways, this part of me is also dying hard. Add a few searing, hurtful comments in there by outsiders along the way, and you have an ongoing mental hotbed of personal judgment.

It sounds silly, but I've started small to try to get some sort of self-love back. I struggle even with the term *self-love* because Christendom doesn't exactly support it, at least not in the way many of us think, and I tend to agree with that camp in this sense: loving ourselves too much has gotten a whole lot of us in trouble. It got Eve in trouble, too, and every person since.

I'm not talking about indulgence, though, just as I'm not talking about going too far the other way and not loving yourself at all and treating yourself unkindly. That's what people like me, who can be too strict with themselves, can wind up doing, and it causes a heap of trouble on the opposite end. Self-love for me, at this point, is acceptance and confidence in my own God-given DNA and giftings. I've garnered a great deal of joy since I've been praying for that. If you don't like the term *self-love*, then don't use it, but remember that Jesus does want us to love ourselves because He wants us to love all of His creation, which includes you, so it is not sinful to do so. And there is no humanistic, woo-woo stuff involved in living with a Psalm 139 mentality.

I'm tired of being hard on myself, so I go to work on it. Loving ourselves doesn't just happen. I wish it were that easy. It should be. But it's a choice as it is to choose to love everyone else. The more I love myself, the more I can love others, and when I don't, it kinks the hose for love to flow through. So I must practice. For example, I decided one day that with all the many events that were happening during that week of my life, I needed to make a list of ways to love myself well. It's somewhat elementary, but go with it if you will:

> **The more I love myself, the more I can love others, and when I don't, it kinks the hose for love to flow through.**

- Eat a sucker in the bathtub like you are eight. You will feel eight again, and happy. (I like the round, Creamsicle kind from CVS. But you do you.)
- Lie down and sleep for twenty minutes on the couch in the middle of the day and don't get mad at yourself for doing it.
- Go to church with an iron hole in your dress from an unfortunate morning mishap and be *meh* about the whole thing. Smile when, as you hoped, no one notices or cares. (Trust me. They won't.)
- Tell your strict brain you "just can't do that" [whatever you think you have to do] today. Defy strict brain and feel proud for not getting bullied.

- Make boring spaghetti for dinner, again, instead of being a more creative cook. Nearly cry when you're met with "That's my favorite!" from the people you thought you'd disappoint, and let love mend you again.
- Take an Instagram picture in a before state—but one where you kind of like the way it looks. See the symbolism in what's happening inside you and accept the unfinished canvas as still good.

I share this list on Instagram to a chorus of kindreds:

Thank you for this. The hardest person for me to love is me.
It's a constant struggle.
I'm gonna read this every day.
Needed it so much.
Saw a picture of myself taken Sunday, and I was so mean to
    myself immediately. Gotta change that!
Thank you. Sure needed to read this before I went to sleep
    here in Croatia.

Turns out that, for most of us, choosing love over judgment needs to start in the mirror.

The love of Jesus is here to convince you to love yourself again or, maybe, for the first time in your life. Everything from here depends on it. We can't be who we need to be until we get this. Jesus' love *is* stronger than self-loathing, my friend. Don't let the lies in your head become your truth. It's not about you being enough (you aren't). It's about you being loved enough (you are). Be driven from the place of perfect love versus a perfect life that your best friend, Jesus, offers you, every day. You have no right

> Don't let the lies in your head become your truth. It's not about you being enough (you aren't). It's about your being loved enough (you are).

63

to withhold that love from yourself on your way to extending it to others. Don't bypass this crucial step.

Love is stronger than you think. Test it. Ask God to prove it to you. Choose love over judgment in your next moment of decision and see what happens. Love someone enough to risk.

And love yourself by treating yourself kindly.

LOVE IS SUPER-SIZED

There are different ways to love people. Jesus was the expert at them all, and none was His equal.

Loving people requires a keen understanding of what their needs are at what time—the psychology of humanity laced with spiritual understanding only the Holy Spirit can truly provide. I have played the piano most of my life and still dabble at playing. Knowing what way to love someone at what time reminds me of perfect notes played on a keyboard. We may have the mechanics to love someone. But if we don't have the right intuition, we will play the wrong song and sour the entire thing.

Sometimes people will need to be loved by our silence. Not a word spoken but simply an outstretched hand or being held while they cry. Sometimes they will need words, and we gravely need the Spirit to give those to us, especially when it gets tricky and we are out of our pay grade in a situation we have no personal experience. Only God knows how to compensate and make us wise, despite ourselves. Sometimes they need our presence over time, knowing we will not leave no matter how tough they make it on us. Sometimes they need food. They need us to give their dog a bath. They need us to have a talk with the teenage son they are having a hard time reaching because maybe someone else's influence will help.

Sometimes a friend may need us to love her through her anger over a divorce, even when we have history with both parties involved. Sometimes people need us to love them by hanging in there when they leave our church, and we feel awkward about that. Sometimes they need us to love them enough to walk out of a room when someone starts to gossip about them, even when we would like to stay and listen to the rest. Sometimes love looks like not being mad at them for not answering our text, forgiving them for what they said that hurt us, encouraging them when we've encouraged them a hundred times and it's never done any good.

Love looks different at different times, and we need to know which song of love to play when.

John 8 is a master class in this kind of insight. Jesus loved the woman caught in adultery in beautiful ways, more than just one, and He loved all of us at the same time—because what He did for her then is exactly what He does for us all now. He went out on a limb because love always does:

> The scribes and the Pharisees brought a woman who had been caught in adultery, and placing her in the midst they said to him, "Teacher, this woman has been caught in the act of adultery. Now in the Law, Moses commanded us to stone such women. So what do you say?" This they said to test him, that they might have some charge to bring against him. (vv. 3–6 ESV)

Jesus wasn't concerned about what could be done to Him. His focus was on being what this woman needed. When we spiritually mature into this type of believer, the world will look different.

Jesus held his tongue. He wisely knew when to speak and when not to, in this situation and so many in the Word. Sometimes holding our tongues is the most loving thing we can do. It is the perfect song to play in a situation, and we will need the discernment and power of God to be able to pull it off. Verse 6 continues, "Jesus bent down and wrote with his finger on the ground" (ESV). Later Jesus would speak, but at this moment, He spoke loudly through silence.

Jesus spoke up on the woman's behalf. Coming to the defense of this woman was a loving act of a loving God, and He did not hold back or do so with passivity: "And as they continued to ask him, he stood up and said to them, 'Let him who is without sin among you be the first to throw a stone at her'" (v. 8 ESV). In so doing, He said to the woman: "I love you." The precious gift of defense should speak to our own hearts, not only to remind us of how God handles us, but to inspire us to follow His lead. There come times when we need to speak on behalf of others, and this is a rare commodity in a world that will fight for its own rights but will rarely be found defending the rights of others. Let Jesus be our example.

> Sometimes holding our tongues is the most loving thing we can do.

Jesus forgave. I can't think of anything more stunning than forgiveness. What is more loving than expunging sin? The mistreatments and injustices piled against us may seem unforgivable, but when we look at Jesus, we know there is nothing we cannot forgive. I know some reading this may bristle over the idea, for some things are heinous and don't deserve our grace. I agree. But in the face of love and Jesus, where else is there to land? "Jesus stood up and said to her, 'Woman, where are they? Has no one condemned you?' She said, 'No one, Lord.' And Jesus said, 'Neither do I condemn you; go, and from now on sin no more'" (vv. 10–11 ESV).

Love is indeed bigger than life. It is bigger than our anger. Bigger than fear, bigger than resentment, bigger than law. Different songs of love may be played, but love will be the constant. It is why Jesus came; it is why He died; it is why He stays with us even today, when we have done our best to run Him off.

We are forever safe with love. May we constantly choose love over judgment in this Jesus-over-everything life. With Jesus in our hearts, we literally have it in us.

FOUR

HOLINESS OVER FREEDOM

THE PROBLEM WITH WESTERN CHRISTIANS IS NOT THAT THEY AREN'T WHERE THEY SHOULD BE BUT THAT THEY AREN'T WHAT THEY SHOULD BE WHERE THEY ARE.
—OS GUINNESS, *THE CALL*

My first sip of alcohol was with my friend Brooke in high school, and it was a beer. My first thought was that it was the worst thing I'd ever tasted in my life, and I wasn't sure why people drank it on purpose.

I guess you could say I was drinking it on purpose, too, that day with Brooke, but not because I liked its flavor with pizza or craved a cold one on a hot day. My purpose was to escape the label of prude preacher's kid that I was so sick of everyone sticking on me, and beer was sure to help. When you're a teenager, you want nothing more than to be normal and nothing less than to stand out from the choices of your parents, particularly if they are seen as low-key uncool. I loved my parents and Jesus, but I sure didn't want them messing with my popularity plans.

I never got into beer, but I kept drinking it sometimes anyway. Brooke's older brother would get it for us, or sometimes he just had it sitting around, and we could go to his house and sip it with him. I pretended to like the beer, but it was always gross to me. Eventually other drinks with brand names, like Purple Passion, and screwdrivers came along, and I liked them a little better. But I never truly liked any of them. I just drank them to be like everyone else and to escape being me.

College hit, and my friends changed, but the pull to drink alcohol increased. When my friends and I weren't hopping around in our Baptist college's local town between parties, we found ourselves driving forty-five minutes back to my hometown to the large university frat parties we crashed. No one turned down females in miniskirts, and we quickly blended with the crowd. Drinks in red cups were shoved into our hands. Sometimes I drank them. Most of the time I held them and pretended to, just so not to look like a weirdo. Sometimes I even acted drunk so people would stop bugging me to drink more.

It didn't take me long to realize that alcohol never brought me one good thing. It was attached to every compromising choice I made in college. It never made me a better person. It never moved me closer to Jesus. It never made me feel like I was strong. It never nurtured my soul. It never made me feel real and true. It never held me for the long haul. It never brought out my best. I hated it, and I thought I needed it at the same time.

It did, however, bring me things, like attention from guys who didn't really care about me and tears for when it altered my brain and I later regretted something I'd done or said that was stupid. If it made me funnier at all, then it was the sad kind of funny that everyone gets a good pity laugh over but silently feels sorry for. It brought me even deeper regrets, for times when I'd been under its influence, gotten behind the wheel of a car, and driven down roads I can't remember, putting my life and other people's lives at risk. Even now, alcohol is still bringing me something—pain, as I feel emotional, exposing this part of me that I've never exposed before on paper, and embarrassment that this is a part of my story that I wish my kids and my mother won't read.

I stopped drinking alcohol as a sophomore in college after a train-wreck freshman year, a subsequent summer of confession and repentance, and Jesus and me getting a whole lot of things straightened out. I literally became a different person. I became the Lisa I was meant to be before I decided I needed to prove myself to people. I told Jesus I would do whatever He wanted me to do with my life from that point forward. Anything. Everything. I meant every word.

Twenty-eight years have passed since then. Though it was never about alcohol, and still isn't, I could probably count on both hands the amount of times I've had a drink since—maybe I'd get to twenty. I am no legalist. I have no history of alcoholism in my family to make me wary. I simply let that part of my life go, including alcohol—something that worked against me more than for me—and I don't want it back. It started out as a choice: for me, sobriety in this area was a choice for complete spiritual submission and clarity. I decided then that I could not afford for anything to come in and complicate my life the way alcohol had done. It was a holiness-over-freedom choice, one we all have to make in individual areas for ourselves. Making a similar choice in areas like TV and my phone is currently proving much harder.

There's a basic misunderstanding I want to clear up right off the bat because it's important in how we view and, as a result, make a choice for holiness: it isn't about rules; it is about spiritual relinquishment. There's a big difference between the two because only the latter has ultimate benefit to us, and as humans, this would pique our interest. (I wouldn't typically advocate seeking things to gratify self, but when God ordains a spiritual principle, though it is primarily to honor Him, it will always come with benefit to us.) The reason why many of us don't like the idea of holiness is because we have gotten the idea that it will be a drag to our otherwise fun, self-governed life. The first question I would ask you to consider is, *How fun is your life, really, with you running the show, and how complicated has it gotten?* The next question I would ask is, *Do you believe Jesus is for you and has your best interests in mind?* If the answer to that is yes, then you must believe that His command for holiness was given with a motivation of love, which can be trusted.

Holiness over freedom is a daily choice (that you already make, by the way) for or against divine submission. It is also a choice not to let your freedoms overpower you in their subtle governing that can eventually turn to a radical takeover of your life. *Adamant* author and Bible teacher Lisa Bevere said it best: you will never have authority over something you are entertained by.[1] And therein lies the reason many of us walk around feeling weak and defeated many days.

> **Holiness isn't about rules; it is about spiritual relinquishment.**

We will discuss how in this unique daily choice for holiness you actually do get to have your freedom, but the first choice is to decide against it so you can have it back in greater measure. (I know that may sound big right now, but trust me. You'll see what I mean and love it, I believe.) Don't make this topical, even though as you spiritually submit to Jesus, specifics He will ask you to relinquish will come up. Focus on, as Os Guinness put it, "not . . . where [you] should be but . . . what [you] should be where you are."[2] The "where" tends to fall in place after that.

Some great questions to ask Jesus as you dive into this chapter are these:

1. What freedom(s) am I enjoying more than Your Word?
2. What is distracting me from living all in with You?
3. What am I resisting letting go of by way of justification that I sense You speaking to me about?

I want you to ask Jesus these questions and not yourself because there's no risk of Jesus not being completely honest with you. He loves us too much to let us think that *our* freedoms will bring the kind of *true* freedom that submitting our lives only to Him will bring.

HOW YOU KNOW WHAT NEEDS TO GO

When my dad used to say hard things from the pulpit, he used to preface them with these words: "Buckle your pew belt." I knew he loved Jesus, and he studied and loved the Word, so I was ready for the tough love. I hope by now, four chapters deep into this book, you are at least starting to trust the same about me.

Drinking alcohol is an arguably harmless and pleasurable act for many in its social practice. What I don't think is debatable is how alcohol is one of the things hurting the body of Christ through our overindulgent liberalism regarding it (please read that last part again and then again) under the banner of freedom, which, by the way, is what Jesus died to give us—not to, in a reverse move, watch us become enslaved. But that's only one act. Think about it. Many of us are becoming enslaved by our own freedoms—where we go, what we watch, how we spend our money—choosing complacency and financial security over calling, binge-watching over exercising, relationship-building over study. You know the list. You could add a few things to it.

> In the upside-down kingdom of following Jesus, we choose to be holy over free, and Jesus rewards it by providing more freedom.

From my personal experience I can tell you that anytime I have made a choice to be holy over free, Jesus has lavished me with a greater measure of freedom than I could ever otherwise know. It makes sense when we understand how our lives have been created to come into alignment with our purpose, according to the Word: "For God has not called us to impurity but to live in holiness" (1 Thessalonians 4:7 csb). In the upside-down kingdom of following Jesus, we choose to be holy over free, and Jesus rewards us by providing more freedom. Don't try to understand it. It just is.

As humans, we have the tendency to fight for our freedom, which is why talk like this is hard for us to hear. We wildly misunderstand that it is in letting freedom go and letting it come as a natural outpouring of our approval from Christ that the truest form of freedom will be ours—the kind that is accompanied by peace. The powerful prophecy in Ezekiel 43 speaks to the vital role holiness plays in our spiritual growth—without it, we simply cannot progress. It has always been a requirement of God for believers, then and now. And to be holy, we have to be willing to get rid of anything, even things that our freedom allows, that stands in between us and God.

After this, the man brought me back around to the east gateway. Suddenly, the glory of the God of Israel appeared from the east. The sound of his coming was like the roar of rushing waters, and the whole landscape shone with his glory. This vision was just like the others I had seen, first by the Kebar River and then when he came to destroy Jerusalem. I fell face down on the ground. And the glory of the LORD came into the Temple through the east gateway.

Then the Spirit took me up and brought me into the inner courtyard, and the glory of the LORD filled the Temple. And I heard someone speaking to me from within the Temple, while the man who had been measuring stood beside me. The LORD said to me, "Son of man, this is the place of my throne and the place where I will rest my feet. I will live here forever among the people of Israel. They and their kings will not defile my holy name any longer by their adulterous worship of other gods or by honoring the relics of their kings who have died. They put their idol altars right next to mine with only a wall between them and me. They defiled my holy name by such detestable sin, so I consumed them in my anger. Now let them stop worshiping other gods and honoring the relics of their kings, and I will live among them forever.

"Son of man, describe to the people of Israel the Temple I have shown you, so they will be ashamed of all their sins. Let them study its plan, and they will be ashamed of what they have done.

Describe to them all the specifications of the Temple—including its entrances and exits—and everything else about it. Tell them about its decrees and laws. Write down all these specifications and decrees as they watch so they will be sure to remember and follow them. And this is the basic law of the Temple: absolute holiness! The entire top of the mountain where the Temple is built is holy. Yes, this is the basic law of the Temple. (vv. 1–12)

Absolute holiness. The basic law of the temple then. The requirement of Jesus now. The choice to uncomplicate our life by doing it God's way. I fall short of this so many days. But I will continue to check myself and see where I am so I can live that Jesus-over-everything life. I ask myself these questions when I'm faced with things I *can* do but am not sure help me in my holiness pursuit:

1. Is this a Jesus-first choice or a me-first choice?
2. Will this choice help me become more like Christ?

Some things will fall in the cracks. Discernment is required for those. As we long to choose holiness over freedom as part of a Jesus-over-everything life, here are some guidelines to consider, to take us to that place instead of moving us away from it:

1. Choose sobriety from anything that you use to escape reality or to numb yourself.
2. Refrain from doing anything that takes you back or keeps you mentally in a sinful state of mind.
3. Refuse to participate in anything that goes against the Word.
4. Give up anything that takes time away from a pursuit of holy living.
5. Don't settle for anything that mimics or manufactures true joy and fulfillment from Jesus.

This is not about Christians making up our own rules as we go along or adhering to a certain denominational standard, nor is it rebelling against one. It is not about telling someone else what she is supposed to abstain from in her life but letting Jesus do the convicting. Wisdom doesn't take sides with either legalism or liberalism—it holds its ground. You do what Jesus tells you to do and don't make excuses for it. Even when the topic is unpopular. And I'll do the same.

For both of us, the pursuit of absolute holiness is the goal.

FREEDOM

A note about this chapter: I've earnestly asked Jesus to help me stay in a deep heart place and not a heady, theological, or opinionated place because I'm not your Holy Spirit. I have full confidence that the Spirit living inside you can take care of getting your attention about the things the two of you need to address. Just remember as you read that holiness is about sacrificial devotion resulting in consecration to

> **Holiness is about sacrificial devotion resulting in consecration to God.**

God, and just because a freedom is allowed doesn't mean it will make us more like Jesus, which is the point here. Holiness over freedom is what this chapter is about, not personal habits or preferences. It is what one aspect of living the Jesus-over-everything life looks like in daily terms, and it is also what makes our life less complicated.

Back in 2011, I had just released my book called {W}hole, and the level of fraudulence I felt for having released a book on wholeness was suffocating. I was feeling more exposed, vulnerable, and broken than ever after having talked about my father's public ministry fall in such a raw way. I was on the verge of quitting ministry, and there wasn't a thing within me that made me want to stay. I told Jesus my exit strategy. He told me to go socially dark for thirty days and spend dedicated time with Him. It was a most inconvenient time, coming on the heels of a new book release, but, for once, I didn't argue.

At the time I was consistently blogging, and I felt compelled to let my readers know I would be missing from cyberspace for at least a month. I sat down to pour out what Jesus was saying to me, raw and in real time, and the words spilled out. Before I knew it, I had typed a two-page *Jesus Calling*-type manifesto, with holy exhortations such as "Have integrity, even when it costs you something else," "When you feel Me messing with you, let Me," and "Say no to things your freedom allows but at the end of the day won't make you more holy."[3] It was from Him to me, and it was for the body of Christ.

Jesus and I did work during those next thirty days, and being with Him in a focused state convinced me once again that my daily distractions had compromised our bond. I uncovered what was at the core of my wanting to quit, and the insights eventually made their way into my next book (tangible proof that I, in fact, clearly didn't quit my writing and ministry). Many things Jesus said to me in that two-page manifesto of sorts lingered, especially the part about saying no to things my freedom allows but at the end of the day won't make me more holy. I chewed on that the longest because if there's one thing I feel in Christ, it is beautifully, truly free.

But in that freedom I also don't feel I can just do whatever I want. If nothing else, I love Jesus more than that, though at times, my actions prove otherwise. There are countless things our freedom allows, especially when you are grown. I found myself saying this a lot after I turned forty, *I'm grown*, in almost every situation, as if to tell people to back off and let me do what I wanted because I had lived long enough to earn it. But one day when I said it, it sounded like a selfish and hollow excuse, and now I don't say it as much. Our freedom is a gift, but it will allow for things without the conscience and heart to determine their value or detriment. It will give us more leeway than we need. So, it is still up to us to use this gift in the way

God intends, and it is to be enjoyed under the covering of our priority of consecration.

There's a vast difference between freedom *from* and freedom *of*, and we need Jesus to help us understand not only the magnitude of our freedom but also how to use it well. Freedom *from* something is a breaking away, and in the sense that we are free from legalism, this is true. ("So it is clear that no one can be made right with God by trying to keep the law. For the Scriptures say, 'It is through faith that a righteous person has life.' This way of faith is very different from the way of law, which says, 'It is through obeying the law that a person has life'" Galatians 3:11–12.) This freedom is the divorcing of an unhealthy spiritual mind-set where judgment and shame reign, and that's not of God.

> **We need Jesus to help us understand not only the magnitude of our freedom but also how to use it well.**

Freedom *of* the flesh is doing what we want, when we want, whereas freedom of the Spirit is living a Spirit-led, Spirit-controlled life:

> So now there is no condemnation for those who belong to Christ Jesus. And because you belong to him, the power of the life-giving Spirit has freed you from the power of sin that leads to death. The law of Moses was unable to save us because of the weakness of our sinful nature. So God did what the law could not do. He sent his own Son in a body like the bodies we sinners have. And in that body God declared an end to sin's control over us by giving his Son as a sacrifice for our sins. He did this so that the just requirement of the law would be fully satisfied for us, who no longer follow our sinful nature but instead follow the Spirit. (Romans 8:1–4)

When we live in the freedom *of* and in the Spirit, we are freed from the grip of sin that once held us, and in that we are free to do what we choose, but we begin to choose differently under this influence. It is not a free-for-all with the personal branding of *I'm grown*. It is the beautiful responsibility of a Holy Spirit–guided autonomy. The irony of the Christian faith is that we live a humanly free-will, free-choice life. And yet we are called to simultaneously live a spiritual life of complete dependence.

As believers, because of our free will, we can either live in freedom of the flesh or of the Spirit. Yes, we can still make flesh decisions even when we are saved and do so, every day. We are not robots. It's important to understand these things about freedom so we don't abuse or misuse it as we tend to do with other Christian cornerstones, like grace. Our freedom is not an umbrella that covers all behavior, good or bad. It is not to be the card we play so we don't have to own our choices. For some of us, it's been the flag we've waved our entire lives. No one wants to be a legalist, and everyone likes the idea of doing what we want, so freedom is an easy sell to get people out of our business.

But the holiness-over-freedom lifestyle we are talking about that leads us into a Jesus-over-everything life is not a freedom from legalism. (That's a given. That is right and good.) It is the freedom of the flesh versus of the Spirit, and we choose which source will run our life. The freedom of the flesh will be governed by you and will result in a predominantly self-run life. The freedom of the Spirit will be governed by God and will ultimately be a choice for holiness.

Peek back at those two lands in chapter 1—the complicated land of the deadly overs and the untangled, Jesus-over-everything land, where priorities are correctly ordered. Perhaps nothing brings more complication than the chaos our own free choices can bring us. All our overdoing—the things we decide we have a license to do and that become our only guidelines as we dive, willingly and headfirst, into a mess. But when our freedom is

> The irony of the Christian faith is that we live a humanly free-will, free-choice life. And yet we are called to simultaneously live a spiritual life of complete dependence.

regulated by Jesus, we are exhilarated by healthy parameters. I've been a believer for more than forty years, a wild and stubborn one at that, and I've never felt more alive than when Jesus has been fully in charge of my life. I've also never seen a passionate Jesus follower with buyer's regret. You don't lament something replaced by something better. You never miss the things that steal the abundant life out from under you when you are eating out of the Hand of Abundance.

And there is that one other thing when it comes to freedom that we shouldn't miss in the Word since this issue of Christian liberty is beautifully addressed by Paul himself: "'Everything is permissible,' but not everything is helpful. 'Everything is permissible,' but not everything builds up" (1 Corinthians 10:23 HCSB). This warning from Israel's past—sort of a "*Psst.* Hey, remember how they messed around with sex and ended up dead, to the tune of twenty-three thousand people? How they complained and were killed? How they tested God and were killed by SNAKES? Basically . . . DON'T DO THAT" (vv. 8–10, author's paraphrase).

It's a good and sober reminder that God isn't playing when it comes to holiness. That just because we *can* do something doesn't mean we *should*. It's more than just picking between our liberties and our holiness—in this choice we ought to have shoes off, trembling as we walk on the holy ground. Israel had the liberty to choose either freedom or holiness, and they chose freedom. They were also grown and could do what they wanted—and did. They had the freedom to complain, test God, and mess around with sex. But from the results we know, putting it mildly, it wasn't *helpful*. Purity would have been a much better look for them.

> You never miss the things that steal the abundant life out from under you when you are eating out of the Hand of Abundance.

As long as we make this about what we *can* do, we will forget about what God truly wants and the life goal of honoring Him. With a self-serving liberty mind-set, over time, we will lose our compass and heart. We can do a lot of things. Our freedom will allow it. But at the end of the day, it will take our life out from under us.

HOLINESS

Holiness is going to be a lifelong quest for us, but we make progress by some daily denials of our freedom. It's not unlike the "I can eat this because it's available to me, but should I?" principle. Most of us wouldn't consider eating doughnuts for every meal. We could; we are free to. It is not illegal. We may have the money, and no one is telling us no. But is it good for our bodies? Is it best for us in all ways—will our brains function well, and will we have the most energy? Of course the answer is no, and we are mature enough to be able to tell ourselves no, to do what's best for the bodies we care enough about to withhold something from them. (We also operate with common sense, which more of us could greatly benefit from in other areas of life instead of trying to justify them with our intellectual arguments.)

Denial of freedom, in cases where flesh would win over spirit, is caring enough about the soul and about Jesus that we deny things that won't benefit our relationships with Him even though our freedom may allow for them. Soon we won't want things that don't digest into greater holiness. Our taste for them will diminish and possibly go away.

First Peter 1:16 ("It is written, 'Be holy, because I am holy.'" NIV) is not the only verse in the Bible where God tells us to be holy like He is. In fact, Peter was actually referencing Leviticus 11:44–45, where

God talked about consecration and contamination and defilement by things that are unclean. The purification ritual from such was a serious Old Testament practice. The implications shouldn't escape us in our modern times—to take to heart consecration, purity, and God's desire for us to live within the context of their boundaries.

> God is in the same place He's always been, waiting on us to come back and settle down to get some heart work done.

Holiness is ultimately not about vices—whether or not to drink or even to watch porn or cheat on your taxes, though everyday behaviors certainly move us closer or farther away from those actions. Holiness is about not contaminating the purity of our relationship with the Lord. Culture is constantly trying to get us to heighten our life experiences or at least find ways to make them more bearable. If you don't believe me, look around at all our thrill-seeking options. Marketers aren't stupid. They know we demand (and feel we need) more and more highs to keep us stimulated. Daily survival for us in modern times increasingly requires denial of real life. Yet Jesus does not need additions. His real life *is* good enough. We constantly feel like something is missing in our relationship with Jesus, and I propose that something is not at all a thing but an *us*. *We* are missing. We are over somewhere else, trying to get high off some other thrill to keep us going in life. God is in the same place He's always been, waiting on us to come back and settle down to get some heart work done.

I am no serious theologian compared to some of my ministry colleagues, and never was this more apparent to me than when I listened to a recent *Knowing Faith* podcast featuring three astute hosts from the Village Church: Jen Wilkin, J. T. English, and Kyle Worley. They were discussing the doctrine of Christology—what it is and the biblical texts and historical creeds that have informed our understanding of it.[4] Like all the podcast's episodes, it was informing and at times a bit heady, but nerds like me often like to wade deep. The discussion wrapped around the topic of Arianism, which manifests in modern culture in efforts to make Jesus more digestible. It emphasizes His humanity, His kinship to us. The historical belief system known as Arianism, originating with the Alexandrian priest Arius (ca. 250–336), was a heresy that denied the divinity of Christ. Arius maintained that the Son of God was created by the Father and was therefore not one and the same, but less than and subservient. Early Christians rejected Arianism, but its influence remains. And this influence, what Jen calls the "Arian impulse," has led to us allowing our freedom to get in the way of our holiness, even in the way we reverence God. Stay with me. I'm going to connect the dots.

Today's freedom-wavers emphasize the understanding nature of Jesus over what we do in our daily lives. And, yes, Jesus is the "High Priest of ours [who] understands our weaknesses, for he faced all of the same testings we do" (Hebrews 4:15); but at the same time, we are sorely off base if we gloss over the last part of that verse, which speaks to His Sovereignty: "yet he did not sin." Jesus relates to us, but He is far and away not the same.

Culture, though, begs to make Him *only* relatable since it's a much more palatable trait. A good old boy, fist-bumping with us through life, mostly turning and looking the other way and certainly never judging. He doesn't really care about us doing things our freedom allows, you see, because strict Christians are the ones who have made up the rules, and the Jesus who rejected the Pharisees and Sadducees is much more chill and cool than that. We are liberal with the fact that He submitted and came to earth, fully man, so He could fully relate to our human sufferings, and in His sacrificial act, we turn Jesus into a peer. That holy and sovereign goodness becomes, then, relegated to a mere casual relatability, and we see the Lord through that lens. Yes, Jesus calls us friends (John 15:14–15). But it is a *holy* friendship and not like the human friendships we can understand. Yes, Jesus relates to our suffering and earthly journey. But he did and does so while still firmly present in a divine role, so it is His relating to us, not us relating to Him. Jesus is our Friend. He is not our buddy. The level at which we understand this is the level at which we tremble with awe over God and, even more, tremble over the fact we get to be friends with Him.

In this podcast episode the subject was not holiness but warped Christology, which greatly affects the role holiness plays in our lives. How we view God and His divine nature determines how seriously we will take being holy, so a lot is at stake. Jen cuts to the heart of our fun and sacred Christian culture when she suggests that even lighthearted T-shirts that roll Jesus into a list of everyday things (in the podcast she listed "coffee, Jesus, and naps") are skating close to supporting a heresy—Arianism—most of us would at all costs try to avoid. (Ouch.) It feels harmless to say in a social media bio that we're "surviving on Jesus and dry shampoo," yet the mismatched grouping shows some level of flippant thinking about God. God isn't asking us to drop our sense of humor. He wants us to enjoy our life but take holiness seriously at the same time. And if one has to go, it can't be holiness.

> How we view God and His divine nature determines how seriously we will take being holy.

I shared once with my friend Mae how God had spoken to my heart about things that were coming between Him and me. She said she was struggling with her great love for a Netflix program that a good friend of hers had suggested might not be the best show for Mae to watch. But Mae felt entitled to her freedom to watch it, so she had continued watching. I told her that one day, out of the blue, God spoke to my heart, asking, *When I reveal something to you that comes between us, do you pursue getting rid of it, or do you justify keeping it for as long as possible?* I knew it wasn't a rhetorical question, and hearing it that day as I related it to her, Mae didn't feel it was a rhetorical question to her either. It took Mae a few weeks, but she turned off the Netflix show and never watched it again, not to please her friend who mentioned the show in the first place or me but because she was convicted by her answer to the question the Lord had originally posed to me.

Jesus will speak to your heart about things—like my shopping fast and Mae's Netflix show—if you are open to hear. The two of you get to decide what to do next. (He runs things, but you have to be willing too.) Consider your holiness-versus-freedom issue(s), even now. If you know somewhere deep down inside that something is coming between you and God, in any season, do you pursue getting rid of it, or do you justify keeping it for as long as possible?

Be honest. And sit with the answer for a bit.

CLEANING THINGS UP

In the clean-up operation that took place between God and me in 2011 that I told you about earlier in the chapter, God drastically rearranged my life. I had already been a Christian for many years, was already an author, already speaking across the country and some parts of the world. But sometimes adult life builds up, and you find yourself in desperate need of truth and recalibration, for God to consume your life more than your life currently consumes you, for Him to be in first place so things can work like He ordered. During this time, I begged Him to revive my soul. He did, through some tough months of tough love.

As God was reviving me, He had me study revivals, and one of them clearly stood out: the Welsh Revival of the early 1900s was a tremendous move of God, one never quite replicated, and incredible things took place. More than one hundred thousand people were saved. Bars and brothels were closed down due to lack of interest. Stadiums were shut down because players went to church to worship instead of showing up to play. And by far one of the most remarkable things about the Welsh Revival was that animals no longer responded to their owners' commands because the owners' language had been cleaned up. Turns out, *those words* weren't a part of the vocabulary of spiritually renewed hearts. The people of the Welsh Revival didn't lose their vocabulary in this mighty move of God. They gained the language of a pure heart.

When we decide to follow Jesus, life is no longer about our liberties. It is about our responsibilities to Him. It is not about our cans. It is about our want-tos. And in that healthy relationship with Jesus, liberties live at peace with convictions; there is no constant war—we are still doing what we want. Our wants are just different.

> In that healthy relationship with Jesus, liberties live at peace with convictions; there is no constant war—we are still doing what we want. Our wants are just different.

As representatives of the Holy, anything that makes people question His ability to change us and clean us up is a liberty with too high a price tag because the result could be an eternal lost soul. Tarnishing God's good name happens quickly. It's not about *loving Jesus and cussing a little*, though words are one of the most powerful symptoms of the heart. The issue is how we've become a Christian culture no longer shocked by our own casual acceptance of the world's ideas. Maybe the most radical move of God in us is when we become offended by our lack of offense—grieved by our continued violations of the Word without so much as a blinked eye. May even this chapter alert and awaken us to our passive attitude toward holiness. And may it move us, me at the front of the line, to see that freedom within the bounds of holiness is the true freedom we need.

Holiness feels rigid and unrelenting only when we are in an active state of compromise, self-focus, or rebellion. It feels legalistic only to a self-centered heart. If only we knew and could see how our Jesus-over-everything daily choice of holiness over freedom saves us from unnecessary heartache. It's as Charles Spurgeon once said, "If young men knew the price of sin, even in this life, they would not be so keen to purchase pleasurable moments at the price of painful years!"[5]

> The most radical move of God in us is when we become offended by our lack of offense—grieved by our continued violations of the Word without so much as a blinked eye.

When I was in my first year of college,

in a state of overindulgence and thinking I knew it all, I hated my school's rules. I'm a rebel at heart, then and still to this day in some ways, but it went beyond that—my heart rejected being bridled. But when I came clean and brought myself under full and right submission to Jesus that following year, I transferred to a school that had even more rules, and I embraced every single one without thought or question. It wasn't that my personality changed—I was still very much rule-testing me, but Jesus was over me and I was ready for a spiritually submitted lifestyle.

Rest assured, there will be times in our lives when we will want to choose our freedom over holy living and our flesh will battle the issue to death. I still struggle with the wild, bucking bronco of will, all the time. It is in our nature to desire to have our freedom and be holy simultaneously and in that order, but in that order it will never work. Holiness brings freedom; it does not act as its pal and tag or follow along. It dictates a spiritual freedom that feels far less like *I have the right to do whatever I want* and much more like *I'm so free in the Spirit, I turn some of my earthly freedoms down.* That's the miracle of life in the right order. Jesus first in all areas brings a health that supersedes humanity. With Him, we truly do live an otherworldly life down here.

If your life feels complicated right now, ask yourself (1) if you've chosen freedom over holiness (remember: just because you can doesn't mean you should) and (2) if you're trying to hold on to both worlds and love Jesus but do something else apart from Him a little bit too. Compromise leads to complication. When we grow weary enough of the complications of our life,

> Jesus first in all areas brings a health that supersedes humanity. With Him, we truly do live an otherworldly life.

we will do whatever it takes to declutter our hearts. Some of us have thrown out piles of clothes from our drawers that didn't bring us joy. Now it's time to turn to the inside and see what's in there that we bought that has now drained us. It's got to go too.

You may be wondering what cleaning up will require—how you even go about making the choice of holiness over freedom from this point on. Reading 1 John 2:15–17 as a reminder of what all this is really about is a good start:

> Do not love this world nor the things it offers you, for when you love the world, you do not have the love of the Father in you. For the world offers only a craving for physical pleasure, a craving for everything we see, and pride in our achievements and possessions. These are not from the Father, but are from this world. And this world is fading away, along with everything that people crave. But anyone who does what pleases God will live forever.

We are free to do what we want with so few boundaries in this day and time, yet this temporary life will come to an end, and the reality of eternity will be ours. We can give our lives away to the freedoms here, or we can give our lives away to Jesus, choosing Him and enjoying the far greater benefits of right living. It will take prayer, immersing ourselves in the Word, and dying to our wants and self-focus every day—the tried-and-true, never-changing disciplines of our faith—to choose the holy path. It will require us to take an honest look at what the freedoms that don't make us more holy have cost us, even if only in wasted time that doesn't make us more like Christ. It is a choice only we can make for ourselves, every single day, that will determine how well we live and how far we take our relationship with God.

We can give our lives away to the freedoms here, or we can give our lives away to Jesus, choosing Him and enjoying the far greater benefits of right living.

Because if Jesus is going to be over everything, He's going to have to be over all things.

Yes, even the things our freedom allows.

FIVE

SERVICE OVER SPOTLIGHT

ANY DEFINITION OF A SUCCESSFUL LIFE
MUST INCLUDE SERVING OTHERS.
—GEORGE H. W. BUSH

Debbie and I only crossed paths one time—at a small leader gathering in Nashville years ago where we were paired up to share a hotel room one night—but she told me a story I'll never forget.

Having dropped her kids off at school one day, she'd stopped at a gas station, en route to a day full of errands. She'd run in to get a drink and use the restroom, only to be appalled at the disgusting and unsanitary conditions that met her when she opened the bathroom door. Once she had returned to her car, she said loudly into the silence, "Somebody should do something about that!" It was then God spoke to her heart and said, *I want you to clean the restroom.* As soon as she tried to dismiss it, the thought came, again, loud and clear. She looked at her list of to-dos, then pushed the thought aside, even while knowing what she'd heard was no mistake.

I should rewind a bit for some back story. A few weeks earlier, during some personal time with Jesus, Debbie had been asking God for some clear direction in her life, and she had sensed the Lord asking her if she would say yes—to what she didn't know. Like any normal human, she had some follow-up questions for God: *Yes to what? To where? How long will it take, and what are the cost and benefits?* Her mind immediately went to if it would be easy or hard.

And now . . . this. Could it be? The restroom cleanup was her answer—at least the immediate yes God had in mind—even if it wasn't at all what Debbie could have imagined. She knew in her heart, but she pretended not to know for four or five more days until the ache of disobedience was so pronounced she got up from what she was doing one night, walked into the other room where her family was, and said, "I am going to clean the gas station restroom." She was not worrying about anything but saying yes to God. (P.S. You don't argue with a determined woman. *They didn't.*)

Cleaning supplies and yellow gloves in hand and the belief that surely the bathroom would be cleaned up by now and she would get to do minimal work but placate God, Debbie drove across town to find the bathroom not only in the same abysmal condition as before but also with the lovely addition of vomit in the corner. Debbie went to work cleaning, at first angry and resentful but, eventually, compliant. As she cleaned, God began to work inside of her simultaneously, cleaning out attitudes that needed more attention than the bathroom did. As Debbie handed the key back to the convenience store worker after finishing, she told her she had cleaned the bathroom for her, much to the woman's shock. When the woman asked her why she would do that, Debbie was able to share with her how Jesus had changed her life and could change this woman's life too. I'm sure this moment meant something to the

> Service may benefit another person's life, but, first and foremost, God uses service to deeply change and benefit the servant.

convenience store worker. What I know for sure is it forever changed Debbie. And in her telling me, it forever marked me. Because God uses the service of people to inspire us for the long term in ways the self in us never can.

Service wins. Obedience wins. Jesus over everything, even our desire to run from what God knows will matter most, wins.

While the world tells us to get bigger, God tells us to go lower.

While people are out there trying to hustle to push ahead, Jesus is telling us to do radical, unexpected kindnesses to help pull people out of their own life darkness for no personal, visible gain to us.

Debbie's story proves the truth about the daily choice of service over spotlight: spotlight may be what we crave, but service is what changes us into the best people. It is the answer for clarity and direction for our life: say yes to God, and expect anything with that yes. Expect, most of all, to become the person you've been praying to God to be.

Transformation through pouring out. The truth is, maybe nothing changes us more into the person we want to become than serving other people. Take humility, for example: a trait so many of us want. Ten books on this subject would likely not be as powerful a lesson as one hideous public bathroom cleaning for no apparent reason . . . one offer to serve someone by whom we have been hurt in the past or of whom we are jealous in some way, and the list could go on. We become like Christ by active participation in opportunities to take on His selfless character. The myth about service is that it is all for someone else. Service may benefit another person's life, but, first and foremost, God uses service to deeply change and benefit the servant.

When I was twenty-one, I knew God wanted to use me. I very clearly heard His call on my life. I didn't know exactly what it looked like, but I knew how I was gifted, and I knew I was passionately in love with Jesus and wanted to help other people know Him. As a visionary-type thinker, my mind could only compute in big terms—if God wanted to use me, it must be to use me big. Couple that with my visionary-thinking father, who would say to me throughout my entire growing up, "You can be anything you want to be, Lisa. . . . The sky is the limit for you," and you begin to imagine massive God-sized undertakings that the world will eagerly note. My zeal quickly dissipated when I was not given the opportunities to share my gift like I imagined. I was reminded over and over that, being single, without children and much life experience, I didn't have a whole lot of cred (my inference from their suggestions), at least in the Christian circles I so desperately wanted to be a part of. (Don't get me started on this false and damaging narrative.) So, I tucked away my dream to do big things for God for the time.

Fast-forward to age thirty-two—married and with three kids. I received my first book contract, and well-meaning people began telling me things like, "Lisa, this is going to be big," and I was eager, again, to believe it. Perhaps this was the time. Surely now God wanted to use me in a big way to serve Him. *Finally,* I thought to myself. I thought back to the moms groups I'd started and coordinated for my church . . . the friends I'd poured into . . . the small group Bible studies I'd taught in living rooms for years. It all seemed nice, but not enough. I wanted the big things God had for me. I was ready, now, for those, and it looked like I'd finally have them.

But God didn't do what I expected.

Instead, for years (many, in fact) I would travel and speak to small crowds. I would speak in rehab facilities with addicts fresh off the street and cry with tattooed women on gym floors turned into women's events. I went to places I couldn't find very well on a map; preached in un-air-conditioned rooms in another country, where not a single person knew or cared I had written books; had my name misspelled on programs, reminding me over and over again that I was there to serve and not be somebody; and in the process I saw things I wouldn't trade for the world. God let me experience ministry, not just talk about it. My taste buds changed, and I grew up and grew out of wanting to be big. I got over me when it came to serving Jesus. God fulfilled Ephesians 3:20 in me in the most unexpected ways and gave me more than I could have ever asked for or imagined.

This is the misnomer of task size in the kingdom of God—that its worth is attached to scope or number. Everything in the kingdom is big because God is big even if God asks us to do a small task. Anytime He asks us to do anything, it's life-altering even if it alters only ours. We can't pretend some tasks aren't more sizable than others because even in the Word, some tasks asked of servants of God were different. (Ever heard of Shiphrah and Puah from Exodus 1? Probably not. Ever heard of Deborah, the only known female judge of Israel? Probably so. Notoriety differences. But difference makers, all the way around.)

Sometimes our service may involve a big task. Sometimes it may be something small. Big or small—it's *all big.* This is not a rally cry to deny vision.

> Everything in the kingdom is big because God is big even if God asks us to do a small task. Anytime He asks us to do anything, it's life-altering even if it alters only ours.

We should want the world to know God and want God to use us in a powerful way, however that looks. The point is not to deny *any* size task God asks us to do to get to that sole kingdom purpose. And to filter all of it through His kingdom lens of God-sized big.

If you think about it, a spotlight in the kingdom on anyone but Jesus doesn't even make sense. It is never going to be ours, no matter how much we chase it, nor should it be.

As followers of Jesus, we should not only know our place but relish in it. Craving equality with God, aka a shared spotlight, was Lucifer's downfall (see Isaiah 14:12–15), and we don't like to think of ourselves in that same light. But we need to take a hard look at the root of our desires and call them what they are. As pastor-leader Scott Sauls once told me, "The pedestal belongs to Him and we belong underneath that pedestal." The way to remedy a massive downfall of our own is to choose the opposite way, the Jesus-over-everything way of service in daily doses.

Underlying the reason we run to the spotlight more than we do to service are the lies we believe about it, making it preferable, mostly thanks to the world's influence. We think that it is easier, feels better, equals success, gets you more adoring friends. But none of these things are actually true. How easy is it to try to get (and keep) people's attention and stay on top, especially in a fickle society such as ours? How good does it feel to be cared about only for our connections—who-knows-who? How successful are we if we don't develop the long-term character that can't come from being left unaccountable on a pedestal of isolation by yes-men?

The Bible never says spotlight equals success—it says, in fact, the opposite, even in the example of Jesus in the posture in which He came to earth and the esteem in which he was often *not* held:

> He had no form or majesty that we should look at him,
>   and no beauty that we should desire him.
> He was despised and rejected by men,
>   a man of sorrows and acquainted with grief;
> and as one from whom men hide their faces
>   he was despised, and we esteemed him not. (Isaiah
>   53:2–3 ESV)

And yet in that place God exalted Him.

> Therefore I will divide Him a portion with the great,
> And He shall divide the spoil with the strong,
> Because He poured out His soul unto death,
> And He was numbered with the transgressors,
> And He bore the sin of many,
> And made intercession for the transgressors. (v. 12 NKJV)

If anyone deserves the spotlight, it's Him, but that's not the arrival He asked for, the platform He wanted to leverage His way onto, the message of self before sacrifice He chose to send.

Kingdom importance is where this issue of service and spotlight often breaks down. When it comes to our purpose in life, a lot of us want to serve God, but we go on *usability symptoms* and stop there. Usability symptoms—what appears to be favor, success, or importance based on levels of human measurement—cause us to go or stop and determine much of how we view our viability. What we see around us has generated lies, not only in our Christian culture as a whole, but in our minds, and we need to speak truth into the lies we may be believing so more of us get on with what we're called to do.

LIE #1: BIGGER IS BETTER.

This lie has been around for so long, sometimes I wonder when it will ever go away. But it's an evergreen (and effective) tactic of Satan to get believers discouraged and off course from serving God. The reality is that most of us will spend our lives serving God in small, less glamorous capacities, never with a spotlight on us, simply because most of life is found in small yet significant moments.

I've had more precious moments with the Lord in the quiet of my office floor, with a snoring dog beside me and the sun beaming down on my face, than I've ever had in a large coliseum during a Saturday Christian gathering of thousands of people. It's not that a big group isn't powerful. It's that it's no more powerful or big than my time alone with God.

Remember: *Everything* in the kingdom of God is big because God is big. There are many days and moments to be lived over the course of our lives, so if we are constantly in need of big experiences to be validated as useful to the kingdom, we will feel sorely unusable the majority of our life.

Most of our life is not a ball gown-and-heels life; it is a jeans-and-T-shirt life. So it's of no wonder God often uses us in ministry that isn't very dressed-up and fancy.

South African Hillsong pastor Phil Dooley, who knows a little something about big things coming from such a large church, once said this: "The best teams are made up of a bunch of nobodies who love everybody [and] serve anybody and don't care about becoming a somebody."[1] It makes me think of my wildly talented church planter friend in Australia, Rachel. She is a big somebody to me—she has encouraged me on more than one occasion over the Internet—but isn't known globally and doesn't seem to care about being a somebody in the world's eyes. Is her effort any less important to the kingdom of God because the church name doesn't spark the same recognition? When we challenge our own skewed mind-set, we see that human measurement is not the same as God's.

> It's not that a big group isn't powerful. It's that it's no more powerful or big than my time alone with God.

We know such things, will agree to them, yet in our flesh we continue to struggle for the significance we mistakenly believe is in the something big. How many times do we have to read the story of the widow of Zarephath (1 Kings 17), who was used by God to keep Elijah from starving during a famine—and, because of her obedience, keep herself and her son from starving too—to believe that service will often be a God miracle resulting from crumbs? God could have chosen any fantastic method by which to feed Elijah, but He sent him to a quiet, out-of-the-way home, to a widow with an open heart. There's not one of us who can't be that widow. That's good news for those of us who don't have much that seems exciting going on right now.

LIE #2: GOD FAVORS PEOPLE IN THE SPOTLIGHT.

This lie usually comes with two impressions: (a) God played favorites and made some people more special and talented at creation, and (b) only big, bright, numbers-oriented things are blessed by God. Scores of us believe one of these two things, if only privately, deep down. So much of our belief is tied to one of three realities: (a) how we've come to deal with heart matters like gratitude, (b) how we've weathered through personal disappointment, and (c) how much we've allowed God to help us die to ourselves.

It doesn't help that everywhere we look, people throw numbers in our faces as the litmus test for success. How much money we make = numbers = achievement. How many social media followers we have = numbers = people listen to you. How many people go to our church = numbers = God is blessing that church. How many people came to our party = numbers = you are well loved. We want to be a part of what's working, *not what's not*, and numbers are the way we gauge that. But that measurement is frequently antibiblical. The story of the loaves and fishes, the parable of the talents, the widow's mite, even the number of disciples Jesus had all surrounded miracles of the *few* or *small*.

It's not that large numbers mean nothing; it's that numbers don't mean everything. And they certainly don't mean *God isn't working here*. Sometimes He uses large, and sometimes He uses small, and this is always His business. We get in trouble when we make assumptions either way.

From the vantage point of a parent to multiple children and the equal interest and affection I have for them all, that God would choose only some of us to be important or even talented and bypass others is not only an absurdity but also an insult. Creators don't discriminate against their own creation.

Everything their hands form and their minds imagine comes from them.

That we think this, my siblings, is a sign of our desperations of the flesh: to be known, to be loved, to be significant. It is not, on the other hand, a situation God has caused while being tender to our struggle. He understands that we are in a daily battle to compare and does His job to help us win that fight through nurturing us with His love. But we also have to help ourselves by immersing in truth versus participating in the world's contest of hustle. Even in God's great love for us, He will allow us to keep struggling in order to grow in dissatisfaction over a cultural system of self-focus that is at odds with a service-focused kingdom that we might crave dying to self to find joy in Him.

Creators don't discriminate against their own creation.

And there is something else we can do to help. God wants to use us where we are, but location does matter, in the sense of being sensitive (alert, on call) to where we are right now. The widow had to be in her right place, at home, to welcome and feed Elijah. She had to be ready at a moment's notice for God's go. Her heart had to be right. God uses the people who are in their right place in a right spirit with Him. If we are too busy looking down the road, we may well miss out on the miracle in front of us. So many times we've made the process far too complex. In the kingdom of God success is simply doing exactly what God wants. The spotlight might seem more important, but it changes nothing about what you and God can do. He and a widow teamed to keep a servant of God alive. There was no crowd or stage involved in that. No one put it on social media. Nothing stops the power of God and your yes.

God uses the people who are in their right place in a right spirit with Him. . . . Nothing stops the power of God and your yes.

I'm counting on this power of God to set a lot of us free from the lies of the world's usability symptoms, that we might be all He's created us to be. There's some work that needs to be done there, mostly inside our hearts, to remind us that we are all deeply valuable, all wildly loved, and all a part of His grand plan to woo the entire world back to the hands that made them.

God, help us detox from the world's lies about serving You.

SERVICE HURTS, SERVICE HEALS

I won't sugarcoat it. When you serve Jesus, sometimes you feel used.

You give people money for things they never repay you for, serve people who never say thank you, deny your own needs for the needs of others who do not acknowledge the ways you've given of yourself. If there's one person who knows about that reality, it's Jesus.

Sometimes being used will hurt even more because you thought someone loved you for you but found out you were simply standing in a light they wanted to stand in, and you were the quickest way in. I realized this about a friend some years back when I noticed a trend. She called when she heard I'd gotten a big invite to something she hoped to attend as my "plus one"; she ignored me when I was not in the darling position at a notable conference. Her interest grew as certain connections in ministry increased, but she was generally unsupportive of my life outside of the ministry spotlight. I talked to a mentor-friend about this, and he said, "Lisa, there are people who will always want to stand in the light of others. Those are not your real friends." And I realized not only what had been going on for months in my relationship but also why the allure of the spotlight was damaging, often beyond what we might think. It's not just that it messes with our own perceptions and desires. It also greatly complicates our relationships in the body of Christ, causing them to be built on falsehoods rather than on love and purity as God intends.

Perhaps nothing hurts more than realizing you weren't loved for you but for how you could be to someone's benefit. Spotlight brings with it the conflicts of motive; living as a servant clears out any risk about it, allowing for a simpler life.

But service of any kind always comes with a price, and sometimes that price is gifts that cost the giver—gifts of sacrifice of time, heart, money—that won't be well cared for, appreciated, or even noticed and will leave service feeling like a drain. Sometimes the cost is not being complimented or given anything in return, and perhaps that is the largest disappointment of all and the reason service doesn't have much of an allure. In a society that is into quick and noisy pay-offs, obscure and quiet agreements with God to *do it for nothing* don't appeal.

Serving is often thankless, and getting burned by folks hurts. I mention this because it's important to be honest about why even good people often pull away. My close friend Megan, whom I have known as a servant her whole life and used to marvel at when we were in seminary because she was a consummate hostess, now struggles to open up her home at all. The years of service have taken their toll on her—it is not the service itself that she resists but the feeling of being unappreciated and drained—very real aspects of service that cause a lot of us to resist working for God, especially when we let flesh invade *our* motive. (All of us struggle with this in our imperfection.)

> **Spotlight brings with it the conflicts of motive; living as a servant clears out any risk about it, allowing for a simpler life.**

All of us who have served God in some way have the stories. We've fought to keep our eyes on the main thing, and sometimes that's hard. Sometimes God has me doing something that isn't as glamorous as what a friend is doing, and I wrestle with that because veteran Christians and ministry leaders aren't immune to being self-centered and spiritually immature at times, pining away for the prettier thing. It's hard for all of us to die to the flesh that wants us to constantly be first. We want to bathe in the spotlight while Jesus washed feet. I don't care who you are; feet don't have the appeal fame does.

A tangible part of living a Jesus-over-everything life is choosing a life of service over spotlight—to honor and emulate God, yes, but also live the kind of life that works best for us since a self-centered life will always be in conflict with the life a follower of Christ has chosen to live (see Ephesians 4:22–24). Hear me, please—it may feel hard now, but in the end you *will* come out better doing it God's way. The reason it is a choice between these two is because these are the two that will be most at odds: the pull of our flesh to be known and noticed or the call of the spirit to be used and in the background of kingdom work. As pastor and author Garrett Kell says, "There is a fine line between wanting God to use you for his glory and wanting everyone to know it."[2] How true.

There have been lots of compelling books written in recent years about loving people, ministry in the everyday, and it is a timely word for us to be present in the world around us. We need them, but on some level I'm sad that we do. I'm sad we need this chapter for the same reason. It's telling that we have to be hard pitched the things God asks us to do, but, over and again, our humanity needs reminding about things like why we should serve. It's yet another way we don't trust that the system God created is the one that will, in fact, work, and we have to be reminded why our plans won't work.

Even when it's thankless, even when it's the less sexy choice, service is the far better choice for several reasons:

1. Serving God has long-lasting and ripple effects, in this life and on into the next, and this kind of fulfillment is unmatched.

   For several months I've been teaching an "Introduction to Speaking" class to a group of college-aged kids. I've heard pieces of their stories during exercises we've done during our time together, but a few weeks ago one of the students—a gorgeous, wild-maned young woman from California named Connianna—shared her story with me: her mom was on drugs and an alcoholic, so Connianna was forced to go live with her sister, who worked all the time and lived with a drug-addicted gang member.

While in the middle of her unstable life, Connianna was overwhelmed by a desire to go to church, so she walked thirty minutes to church by herself, which started her journey with Jesus. She got saved and began to grow in Christ, and she dove into serving in the children's ministry and outreach as she craved more and more of the family of God. Her service and dedication to Jesus sparked interest in her family, and, eventually, she brought her niece and nephew to church, and they were saved. And then her sister and brother-in-law. And eventually even her mom. In the end almost her entire family came to know Jesus. It started with her desire to fill a hole in her own life, but the more she gave of herself, even from a place of her own lack, the more she was filled. Not only that but she watched her family meet Jesus. This is a picture of what giving your whole self to Jesus can do.

2. Serving God builds character.

We are a society of people in desperate need of ways to build back our character. Many of us have lost it with poor decision-making. Some of it has left us because of our compromise. While spotlight out of flesh ambition builds ego and pride, service brings us to the low place, where we meet God to nurture and strengthen our hearts. He may exalt us to a place of visibility to be used for His purposes, but that is none of our concern. His example of His earthly arrival is all we need to remember to understand why humble surroundings meet heavenly approval. He could have come with all the spotlights on him in the world. But he chose a stable. He chose the dark of night and obscurity and smelly animals and hay. There's a theme here to follow.

3. Serving keeps us from the self-destruction of self.

I had a hard conversation with one of my kids not long ago, as all of mine are at the age now that we can speak as grown people in a more pointed way. This child had been miserably self-focused after a huge disappointment, and instead of taking it to Jesus, they had taken it inside themselves to continue to play, over and over again, how much they'd been wronged. It was eating away at them and was not hard to see. "You want to know the remedy for that?" I asked them.

They looked at me with interested eyes. "Give yourself away." It probably wasn't the answer they wanted to hear, but it was the truthful one and the one I knew would help. I know because it's been the only thing that kept me from drowning in myself and returned to me the joy I wanted more than anything. The best way to kill our flesh is to serve someone else—an important remedy.

> While spotlight out of flesh ambition builds ego and pride, service brings us to the low place, where we meet God to nurture and strengthen our hearts.

4. Serving uncomplicates everything.

I can't think of a better way to grow closer to Jesus than to live a life of service like He did. If our goal is to be spiritually alive, serving does that. If our goal is to find joy in life, service does that. If our goal is to learn to die to self and gain peace, service does that. Every complicated thing in life can be found by giving more of ourselves away, which is the opposite view the world takes, yet the world cannot advise us from its position of turmoil.

When we don't know what to do or feel sad about something, serving someone else takes our mind off ourselves and helps heal us. It's the answer to the simple way of life—to serve instead of seek for ourselves, which requires maneuvering and positioning and hustling, all exhausting daily efforts that have drained us.

And, yes, above all this is Jesus' heart and His will and His mandate, all at the same time too. Service hurts sometimes, but it ultimately heals. It heals people by Jesus through us, and it heals *us* by Jesus through our obedience to Him. Because it's His sovereign concept, its result is fulfillment.

> Service hurts sometimes, but it ultimately heals. It heals people by Jesus through us, and it heals *us* by Jesus through our obedience to Him.

The irony of feeling used when we serve Jesus is that we are *supposed* to feel used—just not in the way that brings accompanying resentment, pain, and weariness. Not in the world's terms. When those feelings come, something with a human in the equation has gone awry. When God uses us, we feel full, not empty . . . beautiful, not ugly . . . clean, not dirty. As we serve God, our eyes have to stay on Him and on the goal of true and biblical ministry, without need for repayment or earthly reward or yes, even human gratitude. Service is not about what we can gain, but what we lose in us for our soul's sake—selfishness, pride, lust for power— and what we give to the kingdom to contribute to God's great plan. Serve, and don't worry about elevation.

It is a powerful Jesus-first offering.

BACKSTAGE OF THE SPOTLIGHT

Just this year I've been asked to write eight different articles on various aspects of leaders who have been involved in some type of ministry fall and how to heal from the widespread repercussions. When you have a story that involves your own father losing his megachurch from a church scandal back in the early '90s, you become the unsolicited poster child of this type of experiential pain. I am undoubtedly marked by my experience. I see spotlights from a different lens. I know all too well what happens when you crave positions of power and fame that humans aren't capable of holding with purity.

If you have ever been privy to the backstage of this kind of situation, you can easily advocate for a servant-driven life, if only for the mere fear of what the spotlight can do. But running away from the perils of the spotlight and to servanthood out of fear isn't the right reason to dive in. The decision has to have more heart depth than that. Yet at the same time, it doesn't mean that in our awareness of what can happen to self-driven motives—ones that would choose spotlight over service—we run toward its opposite to save us from ourselves. Jesus can work with that, too—it is a part of personal accountability. I'm the first to say that I seek asylum in service partly due to my deep awareness that the alternative is getting deeper into myself—a sobering reality.

The truth is, the spotlight can be deceiving. When we poke around and see what's behind all that glamour of being up front, there's a lot going on we might not know. For all the attention, people in the spotlight are often lonely. They often question their place, fearful of the next thing, as insecure as anyone else. The spotlight adds pressures in the midst of regular life. Marriages are hard. Kids are rebellious. Health is fragile and at risk. Put all that under a light, and problems explode under the exposure. If you could see inside the head of your pastor, you'd know.

At the core of it, the spotlight makes us feel as if we must perform as the watchful eyes of the world are on us. We are up; we are on; we have to do what people expect and, to varying degrees, what they want. The more we crave the spotlight, the more unwilling we are to do anything to jeopardize it, and in that we will likely come to an impasse with God. God doesn't make requests based on what will make people happy. He tells us to do things that honor Him and further kingdom work. The spotlight can conflict with that. Here's how:

1. The spotlight can change who we are.

   Sometimes, who we really are changes with who people want us to be. With so much talk about becoming a brand in modern culture, we are learning to label ourselves with a single word and elevator pitches and our most passionate one-liner. But humans are complex. We weren't meant to be relegated to a logo.

   God doesn't make requests based on what will make people happy. He tells us to do things that honor Him and further kingdom work.

   Brands are for jeans and cattle, not for people God formed in His own image. We may be becoming better at explaining ourselves in forty seconds and more streamlined so we keep people's interest, but is it resulting in better human connection? There's a correlation between how clever we are and how popular we get, and if that's not your sweet spot, you are out.

   Instead of being who we are, we are becoming who we think people want. If we don't get the response from others that feeds our need to be accepted and liked, we deem ourselves failures. Burnout used to happen much more purely and take much longer to occur. Now it happens at a much higher and faster rate (95 percent of human resource leaders say that burnout is sabotaging workplace retention[3]) because we are now burning out over things that are supposed to be fun hobbies, like Instagram and Facebook—all because getting attention has become another job.

   Conversely, serving produces in us a focus on others, which changes us in all the best ways. When you know intimately how others are hurting, you have less interest in frivolous interests, like "likes" and "follows." Craving the attention of man produces in us a desire to stay concerned with our own interests over the hurts of the world. God is not in that.

2. It puts us at greater risk for pride, which leads to other sins.

It is difficult to stay focused on eternity and kingdom when you are being pulled out of a kingdom mind-set and into a hedonistic one. The Word doesn't say we do or have whatever we want. It says we die to ourselves every day by emulating Jesus, who went first (Ephesians 5:1–2). Most of us don't live even remotely close to this. When I'm all about me, I'm the farthest away from God. The two mentalities cannot coexist—we cannot possibly want to be seen and known and want God to be seen and known too. One of us has to fade that the other might shine brighter.

I talked with a young woman about this just the other day. She was having a difficult time in life and was feeling generally miserable. I asked her some leading questions to try to help get to the bottom of it. "When was the last time you served someone else, and how did you serve? When was the last time you were truly inconvenienced for the sake of the gospel?" She wasn't sure of the answer to either one or why they were so important. Her thought was to change something about her routine or learn to set better boundaries, certainly not to get out and serve, and I could relate. Those have been my go-tos many times in my life as well. The questions were almost offensive at first and came off as ridiculous. But I knew from my own experience that the more into myself I am, the more miserable my life is because it is not how life with Jesus is meant to be.

> We cannot possibly want to be seen and known and want God to be seen and known too. One of us has to fade that the other might shine brighter.

105

Want more joy? Stop thinking about yourself.

Want to be more fulfilled? Give every ounce of your gifts and talents away.

I am well aware that the world tells us differently, so this will be at odds. And I'm not suggesting you don't set boundaries with toxic-behaving folks or you can't ever say no or should deplete yourself to where you become less of a person. Doing it God's way will never require or facilitate that. When we get off on a personal rescue tangent, that is when we become emotionally malnourished ourselves. Self-focus is what skews and tarnishes healthy God-work, not doing His work His way to begin with.

Sometimes God allows us to be in a position where people are watching us and following us, and, in that, it's a higher burden than we might think. And if you don't think of yourself as an influencer, please start because with social media, at the very least, in your everyday life you have influence as well. People are interested and watching even if you don't know. More people telling us what we want to hear, instead of what we need to hear, might sound and even feel good for a time, but it can lead us down roads of disaster and pain.

I've often believed that if my father would've had more folks telling him the truth rather than being enamored by his charisma and status, he might have been saved from losing his church. We often wonder how leaders and pastors can fall so far from where they started or what they preach. It's not that hard to follow the crumb trail. Most folks don't all of a sudden have an affair or start laundering money. They start with the suggestion that they can get away with sin. Their pride is allowed to continue for too long. It doesn't always happen in a position of a spotlight, but often it does. No matter who we are, we need to run away from the risks of our flesh.

I know the spotlight can look confusing—trying to understand why some people are in the spotlight and others aren't and if God has exalted them there or if it is pure hustle. I'm not sure that is a worthy conversation because these are things we may never know. What we need to be concerned with is what *we* will do in any and every situation, to be content wherever He calls, to make much of Him in every season, and to identify with Him as the greatest servant who ever lived. These are goals for us all.

"DETIRE" AND PIVOT

I hope you need no convincing that service is where Jesus wants us because it's where He lived, and we learn from His example. Everything He came to earth to do is our literal living blueprint for our how, what, and why. Service over spotlight isn't even a necessary conversation when we focus on the will and heart of God—what He did and what He would have us do too. We love Him so much we want to follow suit.

It also isn't a close call in having the true desire of our hearts. I think about what most of us want—to have influence, to matter on earth— the wrong ways we go about seeking such significance and the irony by which we attain it. We will never get our hearts' desires by racing to stand in the light or getting people to notice and like us, even with silly social media followers. We get it by following the words of Jesus:

"Whoever wants to be a leader among you must be your servant,
and whoever wants to be first among you must become your slave.
For even the Son of Man came not to be served but to serve others
and to give his life as a ransom for many." (Matthew 20:26–28)

Jesus said this in a teachable moment to His disciples, cutting through a mother's seemingly noble ask about her sons to address the true struggle—the draw of their flesh and societal rules of first—to show how, as His followers, they would need to do life differently.

Then the mother of James and John, the sons of Zebedee, came to Jesus with her sons. She knelt respectfully to ask a favor. "What is your request?" he asked.

She replied, "In your Kingdom, please let my two sons sit in places of honor next to you, one on your right and the other on your left."

But Jesus answered by saying to them, "You don't know what you are asking! Are you able to drink from the bitter cup of suffering I am about to drink?"

"Oh yes," they replied, "we are able!"

Jesus told them, "You will indeed drink from my bitter cup. But I have no right to say who will sit on my right or my left. My Father has prepared those places for the ones he has chosen."

When the ten other disciples heard what James and John had asked, they were indignant. But Jesus called them together and said, "You know that the rulers in this world lord it over their people, and officials flaunt their authority over those under them. But among you it will be different. Whoever wants to be a leader among you must be your servant." (Matthew 20:20–26)

What we want can't be found in our scramble to be seen. It is found in a life of self-depletion for the greater good of the gospel. And at the same time, please don't misunderstand: God has given us gifts to use, and sometimes those gifts will be more out front and visible, and there's no apology in that. Wanting to exercise your gifts is not self-serving. Wanting people to love you because of it is. It's an important distinction, one often misunderstood and misinterpreted by folks, especially toward women who have more assertive leadership giftings.

I've personally seen organizations overlook using capable young leaders because they were misdiagnosed as power-hungry when, in fact, they were simply passionate to use their God-given gifts. As mature believers, we are responsible to be wise in this, give careful consideration, and not assume or write off someone at the first sign of charisma. We can be very active in service that also has people's attention—it makes sense that the type of giftings God often uses to speak on a global basis would carry a special anointing of magnetism. We should pray a bit extra for those who have it and come alongside them—that God might preserve and keep humble those who have this godly gift in a culture that would feed their egos. It is not only unwise but also unspiritual to assume someone in that place does not have a servant's heart. Only God can truly know.

Ultimately, in all of us, the heart for service won't come from persuasive speeches or mopping floors. It will come from the desire to be like Christ. The more we serve, the more natural this becomes, the more we desire it on our own, and the less we have to be convinced.

The better insight is realizing why serving often goes sideways and how to stay in the serving mind-set for the long haul so we can actually have some long-term success. Some of the saddest words I've ever heard were from an older couple who once told me they had "put in their time with the church" and now deserved to lie on a beach somewhere and just relax. This is the mind-set we develop when we don't take necessary sabbaticals along the way and burn out to the point we feel we deserve to be done. It's also where we land when we somehow make service about us. Service only stays pure when we stay out of it.

> Wanting to exercise your gifts is not self-serving. Wanting people to love you because of it is.

The way Jesus intended service to operate does not involve our preferences. It involves our unregulated yes and our ongoing obedience to a cause greater than self-desire or preservation. We don't have a say in how we feel about it. We have input in how we stay committed to it and how healthy we carry it out. In that, we need to deal with the two things that cause us to run the opposite way: misunderstanding God's plan for service and making it too much about the specifics. Both of these are rooted in our own ideas and ultimately, yes, self. Here's the truth:

1. We don't retire from serving God.

It is a lifetime commitment. Therefore, rather than a *retirement* plan, we need a "detirement" plan. (Yes, I made up "detire/detirement." As my family can tell you, I have been known to make up words on occasion.) The idea that one day we will be finished, Jesus will tell us we have done enough, and we will deserve to just relax doesn't come from a spiritually correct mind-set.

> Service involves our unregulated yes and our ongoing obedience to a cause greater than self-desire or preservation.

When Jesus feels we have done enough, our cue will be clear: He will take us on to heaven. Then we'll know our service down here is done and He no longer wants to use us, physically, for an earthly purpose. Until that time we can safely conclude we are still needed for service.

In which case a detirement plan must be put into place. Otherwise, our unwillingness to do so may cause an early exit from serving God. Many early exits from ministry have happened because of an unwillingness to set healthy boundaries with people or, perhaps, because rest was never valued as part of the detirement plan. When we understand that longevity for serving God is the goal, we don't make unwise short-term decisions—with our health, our relationships, or flash-in-the-pan ministry opportunities that make us feel or look good.

A wise detirement plan will involve the trinity of ministry success: accountability (community), boundaries, and Sabbath rest. Our heart will be much more apt to stay in the right place if we practice these, and service will be sustainable for the long haul, as God intends.

2. There are times we need to pivot in how we are serving.

One of the biggest misconceptions about service is that if we aren't serving where we've always been or where we prefer, we aren't in the right place. Maybe God is through with us. Maybe we don't have that special kingdom touch that others have. We aren't successful, or we aren't being blessed by God. Our response in times like these is often to either stop serving altogether while we lick our wounds and overanalyze what went wrong or keep serving in a capacity after God has made clear He wants us to move on to serve somewhere else. How badly we need to get out of the way and understand God's plans to use us are, at the core, never about us. They are about Him and sovereign intricacies we cannot understand.

Rewind to the story of the widow at Zarepath and look at the main player, Elijah. Perhaps no one in all of Scripture was as pliable and willing to shift on God's go. The stories in 1 Kings 17–19, besides being some of my favorite in all of the Bible, are a bunch of *go here now and do this* and *now go here*. There is a constant theme of God's prompting and movement and Elijah's faithful response.

Then the LORD said to Elijah, "Go to the east and hide by Kerith Brook." (1 Kings 17:2–3)

Then the LORD said to Elijah, "Go and live in the village of Zarephath." (v. 8)

The LORD said to Elijah, "Go and present yourself to King Ahab." (1 Kings 18:1)

And I'm not even to the real good stuff of chapter 18 yet. (For some amazing spiritual inspiration, please read that chapter.) I could go on about Elijah and staying open to God's *go*, but you get the idea. More times than not, we don't serve God in the same place our whole lives.

I've shared in previous writing that when we shut down Thrive Church, the church my husband and I planted and pastored for thirteen months, one of my greatest revelations and reliefs was waking up the morning after and realizing my service to God was not over. That from that point forward I was still going to serve God. I was going to serve Him forever. In that way nothing had changed. God's plan for me was to be His servant, and though the location and situation would look different, the mission remained the same.

> **If you hang on to where He used you before, you say no to the goodness of what lies ahead.**

Your location and situation are bound to change many times in your service to God through the years. You'll move. You'll be in a different season of life. Your new house will take you to a different part of the city. Your new job will have you interacting with new folks, and your church will have a fresh emphasis and ministries to match. You may get sick and not be able to serve like you did years or months ago. So you pivot. You simply find a new way to serve that works now, and you do it with all your heart.

There doesn't have to be a massive heart breakdown about this and a big deal made over what was that no longer is. Mourn it if you need, then move on. Today is a beautiful day with a new opportunity to see what Jesus wants to use your life to do. Let Him surprise you with new joys that come from the age-old plan. Let God move you where He wants to use you now. If you hang on to where He used you before, you say no to the goodness of what lies ahead.

In all this, remember that the eyes of God are on you—noticing what you are doing for Him, watching the obscure moments that get no one's applause or attention. It's natural to want the accolades now. It's human to want the spotlight. But giving our life away in service is what actually makes our lives better.

STEADY OVER HYPE

Liliana Cruz and I broke up.

She did not bring me joy, and the truth is she never did from the moment I met her. I ordered her off Amazon because an Internet friend wore her in her Instagram stories and looked cute, so I felt compelled to follow suit.

I am not swayed typically by fashion peer pressure, but I was so drawn in by my fun girlfriend that I doubled down and bought not one but two Liliana Cruz items of clothing, blindly and without proper forethought about the actual style and pattern, which are not at all me. Liliana hung in my closet until she got thrown out with the rest of the happiness nonbringers, having never been given a chance.

The power of Internet influence.

It's been an interesting few years with the beloved Internet, starting with the most raucous election in my lifetime, with people yelling through keyboards and families divided over reposts and different points of view. We've become deep loyalists to strangers we subscribe to over YouTube videos made in their eleven-by-thirteen-foot bedroom with everyday chaos right out of camera shot, giving us tips on everything from makeup application to how to sell our brand. We may be set in our beliefs, but getting there was likely not without being influenced in some way by our social network, cyber and otherwise. We don't lack for information in this society. What's harder to come by is someone who hasn't been affected by the wildfire of influencer hype.

If I ever had any penchant toward hype, it waned after 1994. When you watch your father become a "Preacher falls from grace" headline story, you sober up quickly to the realities of the other side of the glamour of people worship. I unraveled this ball of tightly woven heartstrings recently in my counselor's office.

"I'm not impressed by anyone," I said to my counselor. "My kids say I'm unimpressible." After talking through the revelation a bit, I gave the silly example of *America's Got Talent*, the show my daughter and I watch sometimes that was the catalyst for my kids' statement about my lack of impressionability. They weren't wrong in their assessment. A man can be inverted and held up by a toothpick between the teeth of another man standing on the shoulders of someone, and my response will still be *meh* to the whole thing.

"What is the *meh* about?" my counselor probed. "Is it that you feel you could do it . . . or something else?"

The words tumbled out before I could find a proper filter. "I think it's a trick," I said. "Like there's some kind of a hidden string or a catch, but that it's definitely not the truth, what I see." My counselor's eyes widened, like they do when we've dug and hit gold. We dismantled that a little before the timer told us we were done for the day. As I drove home in the quiet, I processed this thought a bit more. It took me all the way back to 1994, when my feelings about hype and being tricked married and began to come into play.

I felt tricked when some of the same people who, for years, had hyped up my dad for being the big-name preacher in town, dropped him after his tax trial was all over the news and he became the town pariah.

I felt tricked when people said they loved my family but never once checked on us when my dad lived like a loner in a travel trailer after losing his job and home, my mom and sister moved to Oklahoma to escape grocery-store gossip and judgmental eyes, and our world swirled out of control.

And, yes (hard swallow), in that deep-down place, in some ways I felt tricked by the man I loved more than anyone else for all those years of preaching the house down about Jesus but never praying with us as a family one single time I can remember, except before a meal. Even now, typing it, I don't like the sound of the words I know I felt. (I'm sorry, Dad. You were still a wonderful father. I know it was never meant to be a trick.)

I dearly loved my dad's ministry and accepted it as it was at the time, but if I look back now, subsequent wounds from my dad's public-ministry fall dismantled the facade I knew and loved, which had created my view of it: the stage versus the at-home life, the fickle love-you-then-leave-you church people, and the hype that holding a high-profile position in a small town can bring—things that a child watching from the sidelines can't make much sense of in her position. What was left when it was all exposed (besides a lot of pain) was getting to see what was real.

Ever since that time I have never believed anything that comes with bells and whistles. I have stripped down every hyped-up thing to its bare bones, including people, relegating them to humans who put socks on cold feet, have bad breath in the morning, and will all suck in their deepest last breaths and expire at their appointed times as I've watched two people do.

To live with this mind-set has been hard at times—inconvenient and harmful to my soul, leaving me unable to see inspiration or motive without a tainted lens. Unable to enjoy things purely. Buying into hype puts us at risk for this type of crash and wound. But know if that's been you, there is also good news in the recovery because the good side of no longer buying into hype is you won't ask people to be Jesus or expect them not to be sinners, which takes the pressure off everyone and allows genuine relationships to form.

Hype keeps everyone in denial about the smoke and mirrors of life, and when we discover what's real, the fall is far. People give side-eyes and exit interviews to others who mess with the trappings we have built our system of comfortable Christian culture around, especially in religious culture, where hype around Jesus is rewarded with Christian words like *platforms* and *favor*, and people prefer to keep the true scoop under the radar.

> Hype disturbs a consecrated Christian life—it pulls us out of the disciplines that lead to long-term faithfulness. It is led by emotion, not faith or fact.

Yet Jesus came with none of that fanfare. He used a still, quiet star to lead people to where He was. Today's shiny Christianity has tried to make Jesus into an image we want Him to be rather than who He actually is.

We need a right mind-set—from the way we see Jesus to the way we see our role as believers—as we do life. Hype disturbs a consecrated Christian life—it pulls us out of the disciplines that lead to long-term faithfulness. It is led by emotion, not faith or fact. From what I can find, the Bible gives no stamp to a life outside of the rigor of spiritual endurance. There is no mention of a pep rally. The steady life may feel unglamorous, but it is the very life of Christ. His own life was one of reliability so we might follow His lead.

STEADINESS: THE KEY TO QUALITY OF LIFE

In case it's starting to feel a bit uphill, here's a welcome reprieve: the choice for steadiness will honor God but at the same time benefit us. It is a quality-of-life issue—not as benign as something such as preference of worship styles, if that's what you think. It is a rejection of spiritual emaciation. Flaky, ungrounded spirituality—being more into our fluff than into the true and sacrificial gospel—weakens our resolve to stand against the true and real enemy who prowls hungrily to take us down. We are starved from the depth of faith we need, especially in hard or complex times. The more spiritually stable we are, though, the more we fortify our resolve to stand against temptation.

Nothing makes things clearer about spiritual matters than a crisis. A steady, secure life of staying put when our spiritual life gets hard produces the benefit of a soul at peace with Jesus, no matter what. As Christianity has become increasingly influenced by the culture, we have started not only to see it in our modernized light; we have begun to despise any opposition. The very fact that we could ever put the words *Christian* and *celebrity* together and accept that as a real thing makes my point.

Actual Hollywood celebrity has a much darker reality than the fame, money, and attention we see, but a lot of us are still drawn to the easy life it appears to produce. We may not crave to live in an LA mansion, but we wouldn't mind the perks, at the very least. That line of thinking has made its way into Christianity. We don't value cost because we don't understand the gospel and vice versa. That we could support or accept influential Christians as celebrities is counter-gospel, and it plays into why we have become opposed to a sacrificial Christian lifestyle.

The ones the world (and our own Christian culture) says are "blessed" are the ones who appear to have all the advantages. So it sends the message that we don't have to be anything but a put-together package of beauty, good sound bites, marketing, and high-profile friends to become the most honored by God. No one in this damaging narrative should be singled out for this epidemic, and no one should be excused from God's searchlight about it, me included.

I shared these convictions with a new speaker friend some years back at an event we were both doing—a woman preceded in hype due to her vet-speaker and high-demand status. I was her warm-up speaker for the weekend and pleasantly surprised when she was as lovely and unaffected as I hoped and, most of all, in love with Jesus. Between sessions, greenroom chatter turned into deep heart conversations, and we were both engaged, a rarity in and of itself with a newfound relationship such as ours. I felt comfortable saying what came out before I could think much about the words or their potential ramifications with someone I barely knew: "I feel like God has called me to help us as speakers keep it real. Because of what I've been through with my father, I've seen what the stage can do to people. I hate the hype of it and all that junk." My new friend looked a bit taken aback, but she was graciously silent as she smiled and squeezed my hand. *Bless this young, wet-behind-the-ears speaker's heart* is the message the squeeze sent. I felt silly for exposing my cards, silly for thinking God wanted to use me to speak against hype, especially into people much bigger and more important than me. Who did I think I was, putting us on the same level? Who did I think I was, talking about this at all, being so forward?

Christian culture has so normalized hype that this is what we would think—that it is not our place to weigh in on how others choose to live their Christianity—that there is nothing wrong with creative and out-of-the-box ways to reach people for Christ and, in fact, there are no boundaries with methods. I wrestle with it too. Shoot someone out of a cannon if someone will get saved over it! Hang from the rafters and preach if it gets people to talk about the church! I've heard all those things, and you could make a good case for it. Jesus *is* someone we should take every opportunity to "promote or publicize extravagantly" (Webster's definition of "hype").[1] But our flesh mixes in there, and the waters become muddied, and before we know it, it's not about Jesus at all. It's about the dog and pony show we've attached His name to, to make ourselves feel like it has a point. Christians are human, and we humans can and will find a way to justify our own preferences and expressions.

Satan doesn't want us digging into this because hype produces shallow faith, which doesn't threaten him at all. It distracts us from seeking to live grounded. It keeps leaders on the edge of risk and destruction, and it keeps us bound in an unproductive life of spiritual experience hopping.

On one hand, I hate hype for what it did to my father, feeding him lies about his exemption from accountability and putting him on pedestals where no man should ever be. I hate it for what it did to a young me, for how it wounded me and deposited within me deep and lingering feelings of being tricked. I hate that it took away my ability to live more impressed by things . . . there's something about looking at the world with a sense of healthy naivety that is precious.

But I am also grateful that it led me to be hungry for more than its smoke screen. I'm grateful it taught me not to depend on anything or anyone but Jesus. I'm glad it led me to the best guarantee that I'll survive this unsteady world: a steady Jesus-over-everything life. The temporary high of hype won't produce that.

I know it's a hard sell to come against the cool Christianity we've created. I get that it's easier to be excitable than it is be steadfast and unmovable, to put off rewards for our labors when this world rewards only the quick and easy sell. But hype for the sake of feeding our attraction to the glossy way, instead of what my friend Ann Voskamp calls "the broken way," erodes the purity of the gospel and produces weak believers.[2] It's far more harmful than being enamored by disco balls at church, something I'm sure Jesus doesn't care either way about.

The bottom line is this: to grow as a believer, we have to die to hype. The kind of depth that helps us sustain hard times in life cannot be produced without death to pretense. Recognize the places where its shallow approach has pulled you away from the necessity of discipleship. Cling to its opposite: the steadiness of God.

And then walk in His footprints before you, my friend.

JESUS ISN'T AGAINST CREATIVITY . . .
BUT WHAT'S OUR POINT?

Yesterday was Easter Sunday, and I spent most of the church service crying into my fingers as they furiously wiped the falling tears away.

Easter is a mixed bag for me—full of some of my dearest and most precious memories of a church tradition–steeped childhood. Mom and me wearing proudly the flowers Daddy got for us from the local florist to pin on our new dresses. Daddy in a crisp three-piece suit with a pocket square and new tie, buzzing around the house, high on Jesus' words that he'd been practicing for days. "Because He Lives" being belted out by a fancy orchestra, half the people hired from the local symphony just for the day. A rich family in the church taking us to the country club afterward as a special treat. It was our family's favorite day—the biggest work day for my dad of all the days of the year.

But in my grown-up years, I haven't loved it. Maybe it's some of the residual pain of the church hurts and the death of my father combined, but Jesus has healed so much of that, and I think I've uncovered something a bit less earth-shattering: I just wish for Easter to be treated like a normal Sunday. I know it's extraordinary in the best way. But I also think churches try so hard to make it special, it usually winds up feeling the opposite. (Not unlike New Year's Eve get-togethers, which never seem to live up to the hype we hope and plan for.) I've been a part of many regular church services where the Holy Spirit fell hard, and nothing extra or special was planned. Nobody tried to make Jesus impressive. He just was.

But during this last year's Easter service at our church of nine years, it was beautiful. I've been around to see a lot of amazing, creative Easter displays—fantastic art onstage and lights and sweet parting gifts and all the things you find in a resurrection service to attract visiting folks. But this time was different. There was a short film and an in-house drama performance in the middle of the stage that included tulle dancing—blown in a gorgeous, free-style movement by a fan—and a live band. There were lights strategically placed. And there was a piano—one of those old-fashioned ones, like Donna McLemore used to teach me on when I lived in San Jose. They rolled it out onto the stage, and, of all things, our worship leader played "Because He Lives." With all of that, even before my pastor started preaching about how it's not over for any of us yet, I was undone.

Not because of the short film, so good it could have won an award. Or because of the band or the fan-dancing tulle or even "Because He Lives." But because the whole creative thing had *depth*. It had purpose, beyond flash. And it drew us all into the presence of God. I never stopped loving Jesus' Easter. And this Easter reminded me why.

Jesus is for creativity. This service was a beautiful example of that. He made this world, and only a creative could have thought that up. But there's a difference between creatively presenting Jesus to reach the world and cleverly presenting Jesus to attract people to our talents. God has to be our compass on that, but don't think people won't sense the difference between the two. Jesus is what will save this world. He wants to use us, but He *can* do that without our creative input.

Maybe what is needed for a lot of us is to take a sabbatical from strategy for a bit. Forget talent altogether. Hang a disco ball in your church if you wish, but remember that Jesus alone is enough. Sometimes the most powerful thing we can do is stop thinking we know everything about God and pray for a radical surprising. It would do wonders for us to look at Jesus with childhood innocence. Hype hasn't ruined us; but we have to fight to stay pure. Our casual attitude toward the gospel is what makes radical life change seem like it needs a makeover.

I can't express something so big on paper, but all I can say is remembering the idea of having a death sentence commuted to life should squelch any need to come up with something more.

> Sometimes the most powerful thing we can do is stop thinking we know everything about God.

Purposeful longevity—in our spiritual life, lasting marriages, jobs that make it to retirement parties—the things that matter and last are the things that we steadily allow Jesus to keep plowing. The land of the deadly overs stays overgrown and unplowed because we choose immaturity over growth. Jesus is denied access to the tending. We do things our way and let a shallow Christian life be enough. Hype fits nicely into that lifestyle. No depth, just flash and fleeting interest.

The Jesus-over-everything land has a perfect hum of accountability and reward, which over time becomes a lifestyle of the richest pay-off. Even in the day-to-day, there is great benefit to the inner peace of a steady life. Perhaps our biggest obstacle every day is denying the voice of Satan, which tells us to seek the temporary. When we get wise to it and get in a habit of doing it, we become better equipped.

Satan is in the hype because it's harmful to believers and complicates our lives, yet it comes off as spiritually harmless, which has such easy buy-in. Please consider that back in the days of leadership freedom, Israel was smitten by their hype of kings, and we know how their quest to get one resulted in their own enslavement.

When Samuel grew old, he appointed his sons as Israel's leaders. The name of his firstborn was Joel and the name of his second was Abijah, and they served at Beersheba. But his sons did not follow his ways. They turned aside after dishonest gain and accepted bribes and perverted justice.

So all the elders of Israel gathered together and came to Samuel at Ramah. They said to him, "You are old, and your sons do not follow your ways; now appoint a king to lead us, such as all the other nations have."

But when they said, "Give us a king to lead us," this displeased Samuel; so he prayed to the LORD. And the LORD told him: "Listen to all that the people are saying to you; it is not you they have rejected, but they have rejected me as their king. As they have done from the day I brought them up out of Egypt until this day, forsaking me and serving other gods, so they are doing to you. Now listen to them; but warn them solemnly and let them know what the king who will reign over them will claim as his rights."

Samuel told all the words of the LORD to the people who were asking him for a king. He said, "This is what the king who will reign over you will claim as his rights: He will take your sons and make them serve with his chariots and horses, and they will run in front of his chariots. Some he will assign to be commanders of thousands and commanders of fifties, and others to plow his ground and reap his harvest, and still others to make weapons of war and equipment for his chariots. He will take your daughters to be perfumers and cooks and bakers. He will take the best of your fields and vineyards and olive groves and give them to his attendants. He will take a tenth of your grain and of your vintage and give it to his officials and attendants. Your male and female servants and the best of your cattle and donkeys he will take for his own use. He will take a tenth of your flocks, and you yourselves will become his slaves. When that day comes, you will cry out for relief from the king you have chosen, but the LORD will not answer you in that day."

But the people refused to listen to Samuel. "No!" they said. "We want a king over us. Then we will be like all the other nations, with a king to lead us and to go out before us and fight our battles."

When Samuel heard all that the people said, he repeated it before the LORD. The LORD answered, "Listen to them and give them a king."

Then Samuel said to the Israelites, "Everyone go back to your own town." (1 Samuel 8 NIV)

The idea of having a king to "be like all the other nations," and to "fight [their] battles" for them was a hyped-up perception formulated in the heads of insecure, lazy people who thought they wanted what other people had, even to their detriment. They weren't bad people. They were just looking for a shortcut. God, via Samuel, did His best to warn them. He told them, time and again, all the things—dear and precious things—that the king would take away. They didn't hear a word. The buzz of their imagined better life was louder than the truth from God's lips to their ears. It's all pretty familiar.

Hype is more than a bad idea—it is a dangerous idea for two good reasons, if none else:

1. Its takeover influence leads us to give up ownership of our thoughts, convictions, and free will.

   Most of us wouldn't hand over willingly the ownership of our thoughts, convictions, and free will, and we take offense at the suggestion. But break it down to the core of what it really is: to be swayed by the culture and impressed by word of mouth and packaged sound bites over a proven track record is a form of blind acceptance. It's not that we can't listen to people we don't personally know or follow the ministries of people who we sense are led by Jesus. It's that we shouldn't allow them into our lives as influencers merely by the litmus test of the world.

   It's dangerous to give up ownership of our thoughts to a person who has eight million followers and whose memes we've decided are always based in truth. We can't afford to give up our convictions because a Christian influencer we have loved for a long time and whose every book we have read believes something different, substituting the voice of God in our life with his or her own.

   It's not just about influencers in the Christian world, which is a smaller bubble than we like to think. We get influenced by a lot of things in culture in general and by our friends. We get talked into movies we have no business seeing, purchases we have no business buying, places we have no business going—because someone tells us it's the thing to do and place to go. We may be grown, but we are still influenced by those we watch and listen to every day—both far away and close to home.

2. Its flash-and-bang appeal diminishes the importance of a steady, enduring gospel.

Maybe the most at-risk element to the Christian faith presently is the Word of God, which should be a painful reality for people who have staked their entire life on the gospel. If the Bible is not everything, it is a fool's errand that we have chosen to make it our life. Believing in a promised Messiah—a Savior of the world—is a crazy thing to do if the Bible is fictional.

If hype as the preference is the way we operate in our Christian life—easily excited by trends and swayed by flavor-of-the-hour influencers—the Bible is quickly going to become a big snore. The steady Word, which has been around for centuries, is going to be diminished by the rising tide of flashier gurus with edgier, more interesting and culturally compatible options. The Bible, with its steady groundedness will not have the same appeal. And when the Bible loses its appeal, we lose interest. We stop going there for answers. And we start getting into bigger and bigger messes as a result of making up our own rules as we go along.

> **If the Bible is not everything, it is a fool's errand that we have chosen to make it our life.**

STEADY ISN'T STALE

There is nothing wilder and more exciting than the steady life of a follower of Jesus Christ. That whole sentence isn't inconsistent. What's off is our mind-set about faith and the misperception that steady means stale. The world is a wild ride for all of us. It is at times brutal and for the believer, defined by color and joy. Don't become a Christian if you expect to live an uneventful life where you drink your milk, go to bed at 8 p.m. sharp after watching a mean round of *Jeopardy*, taking a hot bath, and saying your prayers. If this is your view of believers, we know different ones.

After forty years of living the Christian life, I would describe it as many things: hard, beautiful, complex, deep, difficult, vital, worth it, but boring has never come to mind. My dad almost went to prison more than once. My husband lost his job and was out of work for eighteen months, with three kids under the age of four running around. We've had land in litigation and a home that nearly went into foreclosure and careers that didn't work well and debt and illness and marital issues and a church we started and shut down in thirteen months, and we've buried people we love. This is just a small snippet of our life, and I share it in list form only to be honest and say that every last one of those things happened while Jesus lived in my heart, so He didn't spare me from them. Many people have lists that are harder and deeper than I have ever known. Many of those people are also Jesus followers. A lot of words might come to mind, but none of us would say that life has been stale.

> A steady life is not about circumstance. It is about spiritual calibration—where Jesus balances you even in the midst of changing times and unexpected things.

Most of our lives have been up and down and full of twists and turns. A steady life is not about circumstance. It is about spiritual calibration—where Jesus balances you even in the midst of changing times and unexpected things. Those of us who have lived long enough know that even the life we set up for ourselves can be altered or taken away without our permission through death, someone deciding they no longer want to be married to us, or abuse that we did not see coming. The steadiness of God allows us to carry on despite the pain of everyday instability.

So if you choose to run to the steadiness and forgo the smoke screen of hype, party on in the assurance of this goodness, my friend.

And how do you tangibly choose steady over hype in your everyday life? I believe it develops inside you as a result of two things: immediate obedience and long obedience.

Immediate obedience is the *instant* yes to Jesus, no matter what. Long obedience is the *enduring* yes to Jesus, no matter what. One of the most beautiful examples of immediate obedience and that instant yes is the John 1 story, where John has been telling people about the Messiah that is to come and the disciples who are with John when they come in contact with Jesus do not hesitate to follow Him: "Again the next day, John was standing with two of his disciples. When he saw Jesus passing by, he said, 'Look! The Lamb of God!' The two disciples heard him say this and followed Jesus" (vv. 35–37 HCSB).

The lack of qualification in verse 37 has me convicted by the confidence I have in my fleshly resistance. Should Jesus simply show up in the area and someone tell me so, would I hop over and start tagging along behind Him? I have trust issues, so the verdict is unclear. But it doesn't look good.

Immediate obedience will require that we stop asking Jesus to qualify his instructions and requests. It will require that we don't demand the proof we are convinced we need, and that is hard. All of that must die. But it will produce in us a new ease with following God. It will develop in us a greater ability to make daily choices that support a Jesus-over-everything lifestyle. Immediate obedience is the instant yes, but don't think it unsteady. Because of who we are following, it is a decisive conviction to obey, not a knee-jerk reaction. There are consistent opportunities every day to live out this aspect of a faithful, consecrated life.

> Immediate obedience is the *instant* yes to Jesus, no matter what. Long obedience is the *enduring* yes to Jesus, no matter what.

And where the immediate obedience is the instant yes, the long obedience is the enduring yes. This is the marathon. The two combine to complete the picture of what Jesus has for us in the steady Christian life—the one whereby we have daily and for the long haul of our lives willingly given over all our rights and control. Beloved Eugene Peterson wrote all the best words about the long obedience in his book, *A Long Obedience in the Same Direction,* including these: "It is not difficult in such a world to get a person interested in the message of the gospel; it is terrifically difficult to sustain the interest. . . . There is a great market for religious experience in our world; there is little enthusiasm for the patient acquisition of virtue, little inclination to sign up for a long apprenticeship in what earlier generations of Christians called holiness."[3]

> What if we don't know the good stuff because God hasn't gotten us to sit still long enough to get us there?

A life of long obedience is a life of growth-producing steadiness. There could be no other possible result. The plowing has produced deep rivets of godly dependency, and in that, trust and hope. Many of us don't know how this feels because we haven't given our faith enough time to develop. We've jumped off to the next thing and haven't trusted that God is often silent in his deepest work in us because *He is working.* I do not suggest God cannot work and speak at the same time. I suggest that I'm not sure He always wants to.

What could God produce in us if we were to sit in the uncomfortable transformation process instead of running away? For the record, I don't like this question either.

I want us to experience the joy and passion of a life that does not run away. This, I'm convinced, is the primary problem of Jesus followers: we do not agree to stick with Jesus through His uncomfortable process. We only agree to stay in community with Him for the things we like and that benefit us. But what if we don't know the good stuff because God hasn't gotten us to sit still long enough to get us there?

We do not need hype; we need the instant yes and the long yes. We need the long, wild ride with God. I don't think most of have the smallest clue the adventure we could be on if we would let God make the plans.

BE IMPRESSED WITH JESUS

I hope you become increasingly impressed and unimpressed as you move on in life—impressed by Jesus and unimpressed by everyone else.

Wildly love people. See them as the magnificent creations they are. See their endless worth and be captivated by the beauty of wisdom and goodness that comes out of them. Be fascinated by their ability to overcome and proud of their incredible accomplishments. Cheer them on, at the top of your lungs. Support their efforts. Respect their journey. Admire the stories and history that comes out of them. Marvel at their babies (and kiss their cheeks if that's okay with mom or dad). Cry with awe over their music, and affirm their art. Share with them the extravagant love of Jesus, the One who made them so you could reap the benefit of their incredible gifts and talents.

But don't be allured into the trap of letting them impress you, not in the hype sense. Don't get caught up in the overblown things you imagine them to be, which they can never live up to and may gravely disappoint you in the end, to both of your detriment. Because at the end of the day, they will all put socks on their cold feet the same way. And they all have bad breath in the morning. And they will all suck in that final, long breath that is the very last that sends them to their eternity. Let your view of them be healthy and in its right place.

But, oh my word, be impressed with Jesus.

The One who thought up all this and you and me and the people

Be impressed with Jesus. we so admire and think are the greatest people we have ever known.

The One who is holding this whole world together right this very second, and if He were to let go of it for one second, it would crash and blow away into nothingness because without Him, there is nothing left.

The One who is our real place, soft place, holy place, honest place, true place, loyal place, and eternal place of home.

May we never get over Him.

SEVEN
HONESTY OVER HIDING

DON'T PRETEND. CRY. SCREAM. BREAK
A FEW THINGS IF YOU NEED TO.
GOD IS NOT AFRAID OF YOUR DARKNESS.
—CARLOS A. RODRIGUEZ[1]

It was the middle of the night my sophomore year in college. The snow had been falling for a few hours—an unfriendly, cold Missouri January—but I was not deterred. I slipped into my cold car, blasted the heater, and prayed my way for forty-five minutes back to my parents' front door, waking my mom out of bed to confess to her about my two conflicting lives of good church girl and party girl, living with the repercussions of having gotten in too deep my freshman year. In so doing, I experienced a level of coming clean I had never previously known.

At the time I wasn't trying to make a Jesus-over-everything decision. I was simply trying not to be secretly sick anymore.

Anyone who has kept secrets knows what I mean: That gnawing pit in the stomach from a sustained cover-up. Guilt because of hiding things from people you love. Worry that someone will find out your truth. Fear that the lies will catch up with you. The effort it takes to fool people around us and keep them from knowing what we've been doing, how far away we've been living from God, and what our life looks like without the masks and costumes is quite something to pull off. It's exhausting to be someone living more than one life at the same time.

The reason for my confession to my mother back then was the same as it is for anyone who ever musters enough strength to confess: I wanted a well soul more than anything else, and truth was the only way to get there. I didn't want to disappoint my mother—the one who seemed to always be the innocent bystander to people messing up in her life. I hated to add to that list. But I had to stand up to that voice inside my head telling me she wouldn't love me anymore if she knew who I had become. Deep down, I believed she would, but this would prove it.

While Jesus had already forgiven me for the things I had done, my secrets were still making me sick. It can be easy to believe that because Jesus has forgiven us, we don't need to take next steps to living clean. But truth has to be dealt with, and confessing to the people we love is often involved in that next step. Even though I'd left my party-girl lifestyle, the repercussions remained. Hiding may have been easier, but honesty was the only way to a good life. I knew that if not outed, it would only be a matter of time until those secrets would sprout tentacles to pull me back to a heart of compromise, and we'd be in the same place again, only maybe then it would be worse.

> I wanted a well soul more than anything else, and truth was the only way to get there.

Yet, on this night, my heart was entrenched in a spiritual battle. Nothing was easy or made a lot of good sense. I knew my mother would be confused at my arrival, wondering why I had just driven the forty-five miles back from college after spending the weekend at home. I knew that waking her up in the middle of the night might even scare her. My mind wandered deeper. If my sleeping father woke up, he might panic and think I was breaking into the house and accidentally shoot me with his bedside gun. The weather conditions were dangerous; my mother surely wouldn't have wanted me on the road. The list went on. Satan continued to whisper loudly for several hours as the night kept getting darker—telling me to stop being silly about nothing and just go to bed. Lies, especially ones you want to believe, can be convincing.

But Jesus kept pulling me closer and speaking too: *What do you want, really want? Do you want peace? Do you want joy? Do you want your soul to be fully well? Do you want to walk in freedom?*

I was so tired of hiding. So worn from living a double life. Things had become so very complicated by all my lies and scrambling. I didn't just want peace all the way to my bones; I *needed* it. I was angry that Satan had something on me, at how he used it against me every day of my life to make me hate myself. This night I'd finally had enough. It is what is always required of living a fully free life: we hate the thing that enslaves us enough to finally do whatever it takes to free ourselves from its grip.

So I made the drive. I got Mom out of bed, led her to my car outside, and with the heaters on in the cold of the night, I told her the truth about everything. (Mom woke up almost as if she'd been expecting me—Daddy never woke up at all.)

It was hard. I shed many tears, and though she put up her strong front, I knew on some level I had broken my mother's heart. But God helped me, every step, and in ways that let me know it could be only Him. I drove back to college with at least six thousand pounds of emotional bricks taken off of me. I fell on my dorm bed, cheeks stained by tears, and lay there lifeless for what seemed like hours. The truth had drained my body of all the angst it had been carrying for months and replaced it with calm, peace, and the morning-after weariness of a night wrestling with pain. After a while some thoughts occurred to me, and my heart pushed me to express them in the way I've always done best—with paper and pen. I've always loved journaling, and on this day it seemed particularly important.

Dear Me,

I'm happy for us. You made a good decision to tell your mom the truth. See? She DOES still love you. God loves you too. He isn't mad at you for the past, so don't be mad at yourself, either. Just do the right thing, now. And don't look back. Stay in the Word. Pray, every day. And don't worry too much about what's next. Just don't lie about anything, anymore. Remember how it feels to live when you did.

Philippians 4:13.

Love,

Me

I finished writing and lay on the bed for what seemed like hours more.

Class was about to start on a regular old Monday.

Nothing had changed, yet everything had.

The sun was now up, a beautiful yellow halo on white snowy ground, and the day was new.

To date, after six books and hundreds of thousands of words written and published, those words on spiral-bound, college-ruled notebook paper, back in 1991, are some of the hardest, best words I've ever written or read. Through the years I've often revisited them.

I haven't lived perfectly since that time. I haven't lived without ever telling another lie. Honesty is a hard, good choice to make, and I well know it, but even then the pull to hide is strong. I have traveled so many miles, literally, since this time in my life and heard so many people's stories. I feel them. I know them. I relate to them all. I met a fellow pastor's daughter in a rehab facility not long ago, sleeved-out from all her tattoos—and I knew what struggle it had taken for her to get there to get honest and well. The unearthing it took to pull off those Christian veneers and be *one of those people who hit rock bottom* was humbling beyond words. A lot of pride had to fall off. A lot of programming. But we all are one of those people, really.

I didn't have all the vocabulary back in 1991 to say everything that needed to be said in that 4:00 a.m. letter to myself in my dorm room. We don't need big words for them to be impactful as I've realized so many times from the simplest of words and even the shortest of Bible phrases speaking to my soul: *Be still . . . I am God . . . be strong and courageous . . . you are Mine.* My own words were powerful, then and now, and recently I read them again and, with the life I've lived since, decided to write a new version of that short and sweet truth manifesto for any who may choose honesty over hiding, even today. (Please read it all and soak it in. Honesty is a hard-fought lifestyle, and I want you to be well informed.)

Dear Me,

Welcome to the world, hibernator. Take a few minutes to adjust your eyes.

It's been a while since you've been out here, and it's brighter than you might remember (in all the ways). I know you've gotten used to the hiding, and it will take some time to acclimate. But in no time, you won't miss the caved-up life. Open space looks good on you already, so breathe it in, my friend.

I don't judge you for the years you missed while in the dark, hidden place. You ran there because you thought it a retreat from the pain of truth—a better alternative to facing those realities staring you in the face. And then, it just became easier to stay than to get up and leave. Until the desire for healing became greater than the fear of being honest, you weren't going anywhere. I know it was a journey to finally get here. But don't spend that much time on the how or why you came. Focus on the fact that you are here, now. And in this place, the place of honesty, you can start a new kind of life, the one where you will live without secrets, without fear of exposure, with joy that only comes from living clean.

I'm not suggesting that since you've emerged from hiding,

everything will now be smooth. It won't be, nor is it even reasonable to hope or assume it would be. There are consequences for holding one's hand over truth's mouth, especially for extended periods of time, and it is even more painful to know it is by our own gag order. (It's a hard lesson but a good one to file away for the next time you're tempted to go underground in the face of dealing with something hard.) I want to get to the hopeful and exciting part, and we will, so stay with me. But before we do, I think you should know what to expect first. Part of healing, I've found, is knowing exactly how to eat the elephant in front of you instead of living in fear it will trample you down.

1. EXPECT TO FEEL EXPOSED.

You have been away for a while. It's been warm, safe, covered, almost embryonic. Turns out, hiding is the cruelest of all farces because it offers a friendship that doesn't exist. You've developed an armor of dust in the hidden place. It's thick and protective. You have adjusted to becoming invisible. People haven't bothered you for quite some time because they don't see you or know who you really are. That felt good at first until it didn't.

Though you have decided that you are ready to be seen and known now, old habits die hard. You'll want to cave up at times. Resist that urge by reminding yourself of this truth: "For once you were full of darkness, but now you have light from the Lord. So live as people of light!" (Ephesians 5:8). Nothing bad ever comes from the light.

2. EXPECT TO WANT TO HIDE AGAIN.

There will be times you will want to go back into what feels like the safety of your hiding place. Living in denial of truth and the reality of pain will temporarily feel like the right, best move. But please remember what it feels like to be haunted by your secrets. Please remember what it feels like to be taunted by the whispers in your head that say, "You can't come out because honesty will hurt too much."

You know what it's like to live with the nagging feeling that people won't love you if you choose to be honest. You have taken the step toward proving that wrong, and going back would mean that step never mattered. Remember that you are no different from David, one of such heart bond with God and yet a sin hider himself, who came out of hiding to write Psalm 51:6 and acknowledged to God, "What you're after is truth from the inside out" (THE MESSAGE). In that same breath you must know he was acknowledging the same to himself. Anything God wants is what He wants for us.

Now let's talk about Jesus. Jesus makes it possible for you to expect beautiful things too.

PEACE. For all the comfort the hiding place seemed to give, it never once gave you peace. Not that true kind of peace that you were looking for deep down. It simply couldn't. You always wrestled with things, knowing you weren't completely honest, knowing you were putting off needing to come clean. It never felt completely right or good. And now, even though it's hard to face hard things, it's also freeing because there is peace in the knowledge of no more secrets and lies. God will be there in the aftermath. Whatever is to be done, will be done, and healing can begin. There is nothing that can replace the comfort of peace.

HOPE. A clean conscience brings hope of a godly future. Shame and guilt find their home in hiding, but the choice for honesty is a choice for hope. Jesus never meant for you to live bogged down, looking back all the time. Being tied to those things you didn't want to come clean about wasn't worth the exchange of the promising life.

Don't ever question whether hope is worth it. Just think of what your life looks like when hope isn't in the picture anymore.

JOY. Don't ever forget the joy you feel right now because that's the feeling of honest living. No one in the hiding cave experiences this in the way Jesus intends because without truth, joy cannot be found in full. It makes sense, since Jesus Himself is delighted by our honest living and advocates for it in 3 John, verse 4: "I have no greater joy than to hear that my children are walking in the truth" (NIV). What brings Him joy, brings us joy. This is the great intertwining of a life devoted to Him.

Let's get real: you have potential for relapse. Old habits die hard, and choosing to emerge from a place of hiding is no small thing. But I'm proud of you today for choosing honesty over hiding. I know it was a tough decision. I know tears were shed and the decision has been rehashed. I know you asked yourself a million times if honesty would be worth it, but you decided that you would take that chance in order to be free. That is what you are gaining, my friend. Remember that in the hard moments as well as all the good. Freedom is the ultimate prize, and you are now able to have it. You can live with anything except for not being right with God. Your hiding was prohibiting you from that, but no longer. You have decided to choose life, choose peace, choose hope, and choose joy. You have decided that the only way is the honest way. Don't ever go back on that.

I've lived with you for a very long time. Other people will say they know you, but I know you better than anyone else, except for your Creator God. I know that a life of truth is the only life you want. So I'm going to hold you to this moment, to this day, to this new lifestyle of honesty over hiding. Some days you may resist me, may not like me very much. But deep down you will know that I am right, and I am doing it because it is for your very best. It is for my very best, since you and I are one.

May we never look back at the road we walked before unless it is to be grateful.

May we always look to the path of truth in front of us, but never get too far ahead.

And when we are tempted to hide from our fear of being honest about hard and painful things, may we remember to inhale and exhale this clean air we have come out of hiding to breathe. It was worth it.

Love,

Me

THAT'S NOT REALLY WHO YOU ARE

One of the best things that honesty brings is a breakup with the person you've become but never truly wanted to be.

I've watched my fair share of *Dr. Phil* through the years, and I'm not ashamed to admit it. I've seen enough episodes of addicts of all kinds to know that the premise is true: there are a lot of people walking this earth who aren't really who they are. I've also sat and talked with former addicts—in rehab facilities, not far removed from being off the street—and ones who talk to me after speaking events and share a few minutes of their stories. In all cases I've heard their stories about how before they knew it, their addictions turned them into liars. They became sellers of their bodies and thieves who stole from their very own. I've seen pictures of how they were once cheerleaders and straight-A students and leaders in their friend group and community—people other kids looked up to. I've seen moms who used to be in charge of brownie making for class parties who wound up driving drunk with their kids in the car. None of them thought they would ever be the people they've become.

> One of the best things that honesty brings is a breakup with the person you've become but never truly wanted to be.

In a sense they are not the people they once were, not the people anyone once knew, anyone once loved, anyone once counted on, anyone once spent time with, anyone once looked into the clear eyes of and carried on a clear conversation with. Addiction has turned each into a different person, and though it will take much more than just this knowing to change their lives and keep them on a path of health, somewhere deep inside they need to know *that's not really who they are* so they can fight the person they've each become. Any of us who have become less than who God created us to be are not really who we are. Hearing we don't have to settle for the person we are embodying when we operate below our potential, and knowing that others believe we can be better than our half-truth life has made us, especially when we don't deserve it, gives us the hope we need to rise. The power of belief has turned many people's lives around.

So maybe we aren't the addicts who pop pills or carry vodka in a dark YETI cup with a lid. We can't assume we aren't addicts. I talked with my friend and freedom advocate and coach Karrie Garcia on my podcast, *Jesus over Everything*, recently, and having been a former meth addict herself, she graciously corrected my speech when I asked her how the church can better support addicts. "It's not an us-and-them issue," she said. "We are all addicted to something, church people or not. Drug addicts just show their addiction on the outside." And it's so true.

So many of us aren't who we really are—who God had in mind when He created us and put us together—because we have lied to ourselves for so long we have started believing our own lies. *I am a good church girl . . . I do the right thing . . . I will raise my kids differently, and my kids won't ever behave like that.* All the while, pride rushes through our veins like poison. That's not really who we are either in the sense that it is not who we were meant to be. Half-hearted followers of Christ. Not willing to address hard things. Just wanting to escape into Netflix. Looking down on others who sin differently than us. Afraid of everyone that doesn't look or sound like us and offended when someone suggests prejudice. Can't hear about ministry that makes us feel uncomfortable.

Don't take that to mean we don't own who we have become. We might be these things at the moment because it is how we are behaving, but at the core it's not who we were meant to be. But it is still the reality of where we are right now, and we have to first face it. We might not steal money from our mothers' wallets, but we are just as cold. We may not be addicted to something we can label or easily identify, but some of us have gone much of our lives not being completely honest with ourselves about things. It's been hard to face a mirror of complete truth, so we've settled for half-truths to feel good enough to get by. *I don't do it all the time. It's not that bad. I'm better than they are.* We spend more time figuring out how to hide our truth than we do how to heal it. The hiding may buy us some time from the momentary pain the truth brings, but it does a crazy amount of more damage.

God hasn't changed His stance on choosing honesty, since the time He said to ancient Israel, "Tell the truth, the whole truth, when you speak. Do the right thing by one another, both personally and in your courts. Don't cook up plans to take unfair advantage of others. Don't do or say what isn't so. I hate all that stuff. Keep your lives simple and honest" (Zechariah 8:16–17 THE MESSAGE). We complicate our lives when we hide. This is why a daily choice of honesty over hiding is vital to our living the Jesus-over-everything life simply and well.

> We spend more time figuring out how to hide our truth than we do how to heal it.

We can move to a smaller house, live out on a remote piece of land and get rid of cable TV, and scale down our closets, but if we don't live a life of truth, our life will stay complicated. The idea that Jesus presents a truth-filled life leading to a life of simplicity should be amazing news to us. It's not that hard to start being honest, right now—much easier in some ways than three steps to everything else—but it will require us to let Jesus reprogram us.

I know some of us have hidden for a long time. I know we aren't used to complete honesty. But better for people to love us knowing

> **If we trust a perfect God, we will trust that His version of us is the best version, and we will want none of the subtracted version we have become.**

the absolute truth than for us to live with the troubling mental struggle that they love us under false information. If who they think they love is not really who we are, we don't want the love they offer. We can only be who God created us to be, and if that's not enough for someone else, they are not meant to travel with us through this world.

If who are you right now is not really who God made you to be—if you are living below your potential, if you are stuck in a cycle of addiction that has altered your mind and personality, if you have lied your way into a persona that isn't exactly true, if you aren't as joyful as God promises—and if you aren't living well because you aren't being a good tenant to the one and only body God gave you, or you haven't come clean, made amends, or asked for forgiveness in an area of your life, today is the perfect day to have no more regrets. Too many times our gifts are in a holding pattern, hindered by a lack of transparency and full disclosure, altering who we really are. Choosing honesty over the same-old-same-old choice to hide allows us to become who God truly intended us to be. If we trust a perfect God, we will trust that His version of us is the best version, and we will want none of the subtracted version we have become.

COURAGE

What most of us need to come out of hiding and be fully honest about our lives is not convincing, but courage. Most of us don't want to hide anymore. We are sick to death of it. It has eaten away at every lovely thing and everything we love. My prayer for all of us is that the appeal of a cleaner, simpler life will outweigh the false comforts of staying the same. We make too many things daunting, and that is Satan's hope. That we will run from the sheer dread of what honesty will mean. That we will fear the fall-out and retreat. Never having the courage to push back on those mental threats has kept us in a life that's complicated, restricted, and unwell. So I'm asking Jesus for courage for all of us against that.

> Courage to say yes to God.
> Courage to say no to any part of an untruth.
> Courage to choose to be the people He created and not the downgraded versions we have allowed.
> Courage to do the hard, right thing, even if we've never done it fully before.
> Courage to lead others to a life of honesty over hiding too.

This last aspect of our prayer for courage is important because our personal choices always affect someone else. When we hide from truth, we force others to ride the ramifications of our choice with us. Too often this is a painful journey. Our justification to hide is often cloaked in a desire not to cause those we love pain in the reveal, but it's a red herring. Our truth isn't what hurts our loved ones. Our sin does, which we typically worry far less about, or we wouldn't get into it from the start. The truth jars our fantasy world for a moment, but it is the beauty and the gift for long-term joy— the road to health and healing for us all. So never let the devil talk you into believing the nonsense that it's not right.

> **When we hide from truth, we force others to ride the ramifications of our choice with us.**

And there is this one other thing that we often call love that isn't, and it will require just as much courage. Sometimes along the way we get the idea that it's noble to keep secrets for other people, cover for them in *their* wrongdoing even at the expense of our own souls. Please hear me say this, loud and clear: it is not spiritual to cover for people, especially in lieu of our own healing.

Jesus would never ask us to wound our own soul to allow someone else to thrive in sin. Other believers' personal lives are under His ownership, not ours. We are not to get in the way of the work God wants to do in someone else's life even if it's hard. Covering for people can thwart necessary repentance. The Jesus-over-everything lifestyle is a daily practice of honesty with ourselves and others but, most of all, with ourselves and God. It's courageous to help other people come clean. We deprive people of that opportunity when we cover for them so we both feel better temporarily and, therefore, don't allow them to face things, come clean, and live a better life.

Sometimes living in the land of the deadly overs (refer back to chapter 1) takes on a different twist—we overapologize or overexplain for people even when their actions need to be laid bare for God to decide what to do with them. If the persons are close to us, this can be particularly hard, and covering for them can even be misunderstood as being loyal. We protect people because we think it's our responsibility to bear the burden of their choices, even the ones done to us, which has left a precious bunch of us in our own emotional gutter unnecessarily. It's allowed toxic patterns in some of our relationships to exist for years and denial to continue, and the ripple effects are enormous.

Covering for people at the expense of your soul isn't loyalty; it's robbery. You rob yourself of healing, freedom, and joy. You rob someone else of those things, too, along with radical life change. You rob everyone of redemption and possibly healed relationships. You rob the possibility of unity in the body of Christ, something we all need to be much more concerned about. If that feels like a heavy price, you're right.

Healthy truth talk isn't about vendettas or settling scores. That's just more pain in a wrong motive, more us over Jesus. This is about healing for everyone, yes, even when it initially hurts. Wise personal choices also affect those we love, and there will never be a better choice than the choice to be honest. As we live with this tone, we inspire others to match it, and we attract truthful people into our lives as well. How healthy would it be if in the body of Christ we operated with the attitude of truth-telling in a way that felt honorable and wise, steady and kind, loving and comforting and unifying? Instead, our truth-telling is more often laced with personal agendas, anger, and giving people a piece of our minds in the name of Jesus.

I always find it beautiful when someone starts the truth-telling process and others follow suit. Our natural inclination might tell us it's leaders who blaze the trail, but I've seen it done with kids who haven't taken one single leadership course. They admit to being scared or hurt, and suddenly our adult defenses go down, and we don't want to put up a front and pretend we aren't scared about something too.

I'll never forget the young girl who was the first in our church plant in the early 2000s to give up her shoes to someone who needed them more in our city. My husband had asked our gathered group of two hundred that day to do so, after laying out the vision God had put on his heart. For almost a minute no one made a move. But then this little girl stood up and walked forward, the first, and all the adults immediately followed her lead. I call this kind of leadership an *I'll go first offering*, and that's the kind of thing honest offerings do. We wash in the river of honesty, and other people jump in and take a dip too.

COME ON OUT

In the kingdom of God, hiding has never been a true option.

Throughout the book of Jeremiah, as the Lord told Judah to get right, He simultaneously told them both directly and indirectly, *You can't hide from Me*.

I am an admitted pragmatist, but the word *can't* here is not to be missed. Something that doesn't work seems like a massive waste of time. Sadly, we do things that both don't make sense and don't work for us, and I am exhibit A. It's why we need radical promises of hope rather than rigid pointed fingers to draw our hearts to the healthy side.

On one such occasion when God was speaking hard truth to Judah, He offered the alternative to the flesh choice: the Jesus-over-everything choice.

"Blessed is the man who trusts in the LORD,
    whose trust is the Lord.
He is like a tree planted by water,
    that sends out its roots by the stream,
and does not fear when heat comes,
    for its leaves remain green,
and is not anxious in the year of drought,
    for it does not cease to bear fruit." (Jeremiah 17:7–8 ESV)

The alternative to hiding is more than just honesty. It's living a life that God manages instead of us. It lets us stop trying so hard all the time, which is a welcome relief. To come out of hiding means that we choose to trust that God has a better plan. We can't will our way into that plan. We can't hope that tomorrow will be a better day and continue on with hidden habits. We have to come on out, trust God with the fallout of our choices, and look forward to how He will help us manage the rest of our lives. Hiding one day longer is sicker than any of our past choices, now that we know better about the other side.

> The alternative to hiding is more than just honesty. It's living a life that God manages instead of us.

So come on out from that place that seems safe that you've gotten used to because you've lived there for so long. Come on out and experience what living in the light looks like.

Come on out from what's felt easier but has silently caused you so much heartache and complication.

Come on out from half-truths, compromise, talking yourself out of getting help, and the *at-least-I'm-not-as-bad-as-them* mental conversations that have hindered you from living the life of true abundance both you and Jesus want.

Come on out from hiding behind that person you never meant to become but are finding yourself as now. That's not really who you are.

Come and experience the restful life of truth and honesty.

Honor God, and uncomplicate things for yourself.

EIGHT

WISDOM OVER KNOWLEDGE

KNOWLEDGE CONSISTS OF KNOWING THAT A
TOMATO IS A FRUIT, AND WISDOM CONSISTS
OF NOT PUTTING IT IN A FRUIT SALAD.
—MILES KINGTON

Being sandwiched in the birth order between two of the world's smartest humans hasn't been easy, but it is where I've always lived.

My brother, Mark, is just eighteen months older than me, and no matter how long he's outgrown the bowl cut or gotten out of the thick glasses, he will always exist in my memory as the little boy in the orange leisure suit in his elementary school pic who carried a *National Geographic* to the dinner table every single night. (I can still remember complaining to my mother about the unappetizing pictures of the animals giving birth I didn't need to see while eating my steak dinner.) Encyclopedias were his love language. The-now-almost-fifty-year-old man still cannot be beaten in any form of trivia, can talk to anyone about anything, and writes an award-winning kind of poetry that I can't understand but am certain is brilliant.

My sister, who came much later in life, when I was eleven years old, proved to be nearly Mark's clone, at least in IQ. Such an interesting and gifted human, Jenifer studied Celtic singing in Ireland, paints and sketches without an ounce of formal training, writes gorgeous fiction, and works like the boss babe she is in a mostly male-dominated trade as a luthier, building and repairing guitars for some of the greatest rock stars alive. The last time I overheard my now-grown-but-still-younger sister in deep conversation, she was talking to one of my nephews about different genres of art, and it went way over my head. I felt like the fourteen-year-old pupil, happily hanging on to every nerdy word.

I am surrounded by exceptionally smart people in my family. I am average-smart with a pretty good vocabulary, but even that sometimes produces words that aren't quite the ones I want, and I have to use a dictionary to look up the right ones. Living among the exceptionally smart people is something I have had to come to terms with my entire life. I'm not being self-deprecating. I'm being honest.

What I am is a good student. I've always loved to learn, but I was never at the top of my class. I loved psychology—the heart and science of studying people, but never as much about learning it from books. Instead, I just figured out how to ask really good questions. I came to care about connection over intelligence. Maybe, then, not being the smartest person in every room did me some good since it made me unable to settle for brains alone to be my relationship builder.

As it relates to the kingdom of God, especially in this day and time of rabid information, I believe that God is nudging us to seek something more than simply knowing a lot or relying on what we know or study to unify us with people. Don't get me wrong: knowledge is hugely important. I do believe what poet Maya Angelou once said, that when we know better, we do better, is at least mostly true. A lot of us simply didn't know things until we knew them, and then we became better people. I listen to my friends of another race when they tell me how they feel because they know things I don't about life from a vantage point different from my own. I learn from the older generation who have seen and experienced so much more than I have.

But I haven't always been that understanding. Until my husband lost his job, I didn't know what it felt like or how circumstances beyond the control of hard work came into play, so I made judgments about people who lost jobs. Until my dad died, I didn't understand that kind of grief, so I expected people to heal quickly or in some type of formulaic fashion. Personal experience is, without a doubt, one of our best teachers. Yet I don't diminish how much we can also learn from being students of each other's life experiences with an open and willing heart.

Yes, a lot of times when we know better, we do better. And, hear me say, of all the things we need to know, we need to know Jesus more. Pastor Voddie Baucham said this: "We're producing passionate people with empty heads who love the Jesus they don't know very well."[1] We are reading about Jesus. We are talking about Him. But knowing Him—His heart, what He really would do—is completely something else. We can see in the way we argue down the Bible more than we try to live it out how we don't truly know the answer to *WWJD?*

Sometimes knowledge isn't the thing we most need—it is the activation of that knowledge, the courage to practice what we know, the character to stay true to it. So knowledge alone will not be enough. It is the incomplete picture, the table set but without the meal. One of only two things in this entire book that is a best-over-good thing: wisdom over knowledge (as well as holiness over freedom). Knowledge is good. It is powerful. It is important. We have to know things in order to take next steps. But wisdom is even better because it is not something you can read in books or study up on. It is God-given.

> Sometimes, knowledge isn't the thing we most need—it is the activation of that knowledge, the courage to practice what we know, the character to stay true to it.

Where knowledge can be gained through study practices, wisdom is a life practice based on Holy Spirit direction that needs to be put into place early—the earlier the better, in fact. Solomon has been called the wisest man who ever lived, but when he was just starting his reign as king, he defined himself as "like a little child who doesn't know his way around" (1 Kings 3:7). Clearly intimidated and feeling in over his head ("Here I am in the midst of your own chosen people, a nation so great and numerous they cannot be counted!" v. 8), Solomon made the smartest decision any of us could ever make—he prayed this one prayer: "Give me an understanding heart" (v. 9). And it wasn't a selfish ask. It was a godly ask because of his motive: "so that I can govern your people well and know the difference between right and wrong" (v. 9). Solomon recognized that without the wisdom from God, there was no possible way the enormous task in front of him was possible—"For who by himself is able to govern this great people of yours?"

The backstory to Solomon becoming the wisest man who ever lived would be enough, but there's even more. God's response to Solomon uncovers His heart for wisdom—the importance He puts on it and the blessing He pours upon those who are committed to making this their primary ask.

> The Lord was pleased that Solomon had asked for wisdom. So God replied, "Because you have asked for wisdom in governing my people with justice and have not asked for a long life or wealth or the death of your enemies— I will give you what you asked for! I will give you a wise and understanding heart such as no one else has had or ever will have! And I will also give you what you did not ask for—riches and fame! No other king in all the world will be compared to you for the rest of your life! And if you follow me and obey my decrees and my commands as your father, David, did, I will give you a long life." (vv. 10–14)

The lessons this story yields—to ask for wisdom from God every day . . . to see it as the best way to start off a career, a marriage, parenting . . . to expect to have any kind of successful life with finances, relationships, and in all the other hard and complicated things life throws us—is not to be missed. Wisdom from God has a domino effect as well, so know that when you make that Jesus-over-everything choice, it will benefit someone else.

The story in Scripture that immediately follows this passage is an interesting one about two mothers fighting over babies—a dead one and an alive one—and both claiming the alive one to be hers. Solomon has to wisely dismantle their stories to get to the truth, which requires wisdom only God could provide. (For full details, read 1 Kings 3:16–27.) As a result, not only is the issue resolved, but peace and prosperity benefit everyone under his leadership. The God factor is what makes wisdom the greater choice in our everyday life. Wisdom is a gift from God and a gift to this world—far superior than knowledge, which even people who do not follow Jesus can have.

WE CAN KNOW IT ALL AND YET NOT KNOW

I'm watching two people I don't know fight on Twitter. According to their alma mater names in their bios, they both are well educated. The accomplishments mentioned in their taglines are impressive. Both are influencers, and they both have those little blue check marks to say so by their names. I don't know if the two of them even know each other or if this is one of those online arguments that started from a random pause in the scroll when a statement caught the eye and someone hit return and started typing a disagreeable response before she thought too far into it. But it's become pretty heated, and with every comeback I'm bracing for someone to jump through the screen and pull the other's hair.

There's nothing grosser than two grown adults fighting like little kids, especially in public. These two Twitter right-fighters may have

Ivy League educations, but neither is wise enough to know when a conversation has gone too far.

As I've lived a bit, I've found little that makes for more of a heated discussion between adults than when two things are added to the mix: God and education (politics is the only thing to make this worse). Fights over theology and everyone's personal spin on Jesus creep toward the cruelest, rarely leaving at least one person without scars. And then when you know a lot and that's where you tend to hang your hat, you become that piously dangerous type, wielding the weapon of your intelligence, able to out-know people and make them feel small about it—so gross and unkind.

Yet God speaks into the futility of knowledge that is used unwisely.

> If I speak in the tongues of men or of angels, but do not have love, I am only a resounding gong or a clanging cymbal. If I have the gift of prophecy and can fathom all mysteries and all knowledge, and if I have a faith that can move mountains, but do not have love, I am nothing. (1 Cor. 13:1–2 NIV)

We can know it all and still be hollow and shallow where God is concerned. The Sadducees, some of the most learned men in the day of Jesus, knew much but had intimacy only with the law, not the Person. In Matthew 22, they try to entrap Jesus in a no-win situation to prove His true allegiance, presenting to Him this scenario:

> "Teacher, Moses said, 'If a man dies having no children, his brother must marry the widow and raise up offspring for his brother.' Now there were seven brothers among us. The first married and died, and having no offspring left his wife to his brother. So too the second and third, down to the seventh. After them all, the woman died. In the resurrection, therefore, of the seven, whose wife will she be? For they all had her." (vv. 24–28 ESV)

Jesus, with nothing to prove, then points out the vast gap between their intelligence and the wisdom that would open their eyes to the truth: "But Jesus answered them, 'You are wrong, because you know neither the Scriptures nor the power of God'" (v. 29 ESV).

The word "know" here in the original Greek is *eido*, which means "to perceive" or "to ascertain what must be done about it."[2] The intricacies of the gospel, then and now, go beyond book smarts or natural human reason or IQ. It is a reality unable to be intellectualized by and large, which is the way God intends. In the upside-down kingdom, most things won't make written sense. We die to live, we love those who hurt us, and we believe in things we cannot prove or physically see.

Putting too much stock in our physical knowing is to our detriment—we begin to rely upon our brains to guide us, which will ultimately fail. At some point we will run out of information. We will be accidentally ill-informed. There is an expiration date to all human knowledge while the supernatural eternally lives on. To perceive something or ascertain what must be done about it is to dive deeper than our minds alone, without spiritual understanding, will allow.

But there is more. To rely on our knowledge alone is not merely a misplaced trust. It is a form of human arrogance and can lead to complication. This intellectual age we live in—with a plethora of experts on subjects from skin care to supralapsarian theology (google it)—seems to have produced a new level of pride in us as we wave our knowledge flags in everyone's face so they can't miss it. The more we know, the more we want people to know we know, the more we feel validated when we are sure they know we know, and *please make sure you compliment us on our intelligence*. Kids can't be kids anymore because we've decided they need to enter preschool to work on their GPAs and résumés for college. But how wise are we when we run us all into perfectionist burnout? How wise are we when we cannot see how God resists the pride that has infiltrated our hearts? We wouldn't have online fights with each other if we didn't believe we were in some

> In the upside-down kingdom, most things won't make written sense. We die to live, we love those who hurt us, and we believe in things we cannot prove or physically see.

way the gatekeepers to the answers for all the world's wrongs. There's a palpable difference between someone who shares a point of view and someone who carries a posture of condescension, in attitude, language, or tone. An air of superiority reveals our lack, not surplus, in all the ways that count. At the end of the day, Jesus isn't interested in what we know. He's interested in how we live. We can know it all and miss what really counts.

WHAT IS WISE

I've known plenty of smart people in my life, but wise people make for a shorter list. My mother. My friend Monty. My husband, particularly in tough conversations with our kids. Authors I admire, like Manning, Nouwen, Peterson, and Lewis. Personal Christian heroes of mine, like Corrie Ten Boom and Joni Eareckson Tada. Still, I could also name at least one flaw for each of the ones from this list whom I personally know, so it's not as if I am duped into believing in some fantasy perfection. Even the wisest of folks aren't superhuman. The deepest and truest wisdom requires the Holy Spirit, but I've also known unbelievers who have had sage things to say. The difference is, wisdom without the Holy Spirit will eventually reach capacity in what we know to offer a complex world; wisdom of the Spirit has the ability to pray into any situation, no matter how complicated it gets, and ask the Lord to give answers that no human would otherwise have. The source is what matters the most in providing insight.

When we are seeking to live a godly, Jesus-over-everything life in the day-to-day, the temptation to fill up on knowledge is real. It seems like the logical way to live out the faith we profess—to simply know more in order to become better believers. But knowledge alone won't produce depth. We have well proved this with all our Bible study, small group, variety pack church service/online church options, and that's not counting all the books like mine. If it were about knowing more, we would be the most radical, gospel-living believers of all time. I'll let you take the inventory on this to decide if that is true of modern Christians.

But the real reason we often settle for knowledge is because it's far easier to accrue more information about God than it is to live the way wisdom and discernment requires—a discipline that takes time and commitment. Death to self does not fall well on the ears. Picking up a cross is not a preferable to-do. A book by the beach to learn more about Jesus is far sweeter than Him doing a messy, transformative work inside us that requires action. I know in saying this I seem to be the worst kind of hypocrite—asking you to read these words while at the same time speaking out against the idea of mere knowledge. I can't totally disagree. My personal wrestling with this has led me to this conclusion: transformative heart work can be done through books, certainly, but God doesn't need them to produce in us life change. My prayer for the words you are reading now is that they are a kick-start.

Choosing a pursuit of wisdom, no matter how knowledgeable we are about Scripture or God or spiritual matters, is the best way to ensure we

> Choosing a pursuit of wisdom, no matter how knowledgeable we are about Scripture or God or spiritual matters, is the best way to ensure we will walk the paths God intends.

will walk the paths God intends rather than veering onto roads that weren't meant for us. Not all roads will severely harm us—some will just temporarily distract us or cost us precious time out of our one beautiful life—but none of us will know where to go and what to do without the wisdom of God. We just aren't that smart.

As I think about the things that have made people note-taking-worthy, I don't think about how well they can craft some clever words together—I think about how they have discerned life and been governed by more than their egos. Humility has accompanied their speech and their counsel. More times than not, they have listened and observed more than they have offered a single word. And I've also noticed these things about wise people as well:

1. There is an action to the learning of the wise.

   Wise people don't settle for mere knowledge. They take it to the next level by applying what they know to their everyday lives. I love what British journalist Miles Kington said once about the difference between knowledge and wisdom: "Knowledge consists of knowing that a tomato is a fruit, and wisdom consists of not putting it in a fruit salad."[3]

   The gap is indeed wide between what we know and what we do with what we know, and there are ramifications. We may be the smartest person in the room at a party, but if someone drops to the floor choking on an apple slice and we know the Heimlich but choose not to perform it, what good is knowing how? If we know what the Word says about how to show Jesus to other people but opt not to because we are too comfortable in a lazy faith, the knowledge won't help bring a single soul to Christ. This is the reality of this exhortation in James: "But don't just listen to God's word. You must do what it says. Otherwise, you are only fooling yourselves" (1:22).

   We have to be honest with ourselves as Jesus followers to admit that being notorious for getting fat off Word knowledge without action is a fair qualification for a lot of us. If you look simply at the statistics of foster care, you know that, as a whole, the church could make a significant dent in the situation, but thus far the ratio of kids needing homes versus kids being placed in homes still stands. I preach to myself and pray for God to help me be brave enough to walk out the faith in this area and a handful of other social/spiritual issues knowledge alone can't fix.

Wisdom takes the Bible seriously. It believes what Jesus says will work and attempts rather than resists. It does not look for ways to sit this one out—it is ready, always, to live what it knows.

2. The wise hold a valid reason and understanding behind a belief.

You might say that we all think we are right in our beliefs or we wouldn't believe them—and to that I say, you might be right. But what I'm talking about here is the idea of blindly following a belief system or being influenced to the point it becomes our own. Some of us were taught things that when we got old enough, we dug deep enough to find out we didn't believe, so we chose courage over history and fear and committed to our own convictions.

If you grew up in a particular church denomination, the inevitability is that you have tendencies to believe certain things that were taught to you. Every denomination has their belief systems, and within that, feel they are right and by virtue of being right, the others must be wrong. This is often unspoken but sensed, and it was by me, even as a little girl. I knew what my childhood denomination believed. We loved our brothers and sisters in different denominations, but *bless their hearts*, they were wrong about this or that. While I am now confident in my own convictions regarding all of these, it has come through digging in the Word to come to my personal conclusion. No longer have I been willing to merely accept that something is true because my childhood denomination said so, although admittedly it still owns a piece of my heart.

We don't have to be what our parents were or what our families believed or what someone told us—wise people form their own belief systems with the help of God. One of my pastors, Derek Hawkins, said something that touched me so deeply in an interview on my podcast not long ago: "Jesus breaks your generational and even bloodline curses." That's something powerful that someone who thought he had to believe what he was taught needs to know. Or someone who thought she could never escape the past sins of her family needs to remember. Far too many times, mob mentality or heritage forms our opinions and actions, and even when we know better, we don't have the wisdom and strength to stand in our own belief. Our parents were mad at the church, so we became mad at the church. We grew up around prejudice, so we accepted it as okay. History might inform us, but wisdom helps us form our own convictions. A wise person will pray, consider, investigate, ask questions, and have a reason based on reality for why he believes what he does, not just blindly accept an idea because someone told him to, because it is what he has always known, or because it is what he assumes.

3. Wise people are able to self-regulate well.

Someone who is wise will operate under the "just because I can doesn't mean I should" conviction. One of the biggest signs a person is wise is how under Spirit control she is, despite how out of control the circumstances of her life may be. The things that come out of her mouth will be filtered through the Holy Spirit, who gives self-control—the places she goes and the activities she participates in will not be haphazard and without regard; they will be weighed and considered beforehand. We can never take the credit for wisdom such as this. We don't self-govern; we self-regulate, with the Lord being the One who governs our life. The key is always being under the control of the Holy Spirit, and in turn, though He has in a sense handed over the daily keys to us (choice and free will), He is every bit driving us around.

Without fail, one of the most tender yet familiar topics

every one of my well-known author and leadership guests on my podcast bring up as a personal struggle is how addicted to their phones (and often, social media) they have become. Over and over we have the same conversation about how we have to pray for wisdom and better self-control in this area, as it tends to make its way into our lives even when we are aware of its take-over tendencies. In the same vein, every time I post on social media about how with God's power we can control it rather than it controlling us, people respond with amens and likes in droves—because we are all alike at the core of our resistance to self-indulgence. We know cognitively that spending too much time on our computers and phones isn't good for us. We know it steals real, tangible life out from under our noses and can disrupt the joy of simple living. But knowledge isn't enough. Apps with time limits and alarms to tell us to stop are great tools. But at the end of the day, we must have the wisdom and courage to self-regulate. It's a check in our spirits and a choice in our hearts that goes beyond the parameter of an app.

This aspect of wisdom—self-regulation—is one of the biggest ways our life becomes uncomplicated where it may have been complicated before. When we operate with the wisdom of the Holy Spirit and begin to weed out the things that bring potential entrapment and harm, we find ourselves in far fewer messes. We don't throw wisdom out the window for attraction in dating relationships, fooling ourselves by our plan to influence the objects of our attraction to love Jesus if they don't already—we wait for a spiritually compatible partner to share our life with. As a married person, we immediately delete the Facebook message from an old high school friend who is "just wanting to see how we are doing after all these years," knowing that messages like this are exactly how thousands of affairs have started. We stay away from the mall and stores that tempt us so we don't numb out with impulse buys that won't solve our problems. And in these wise decisions of self-regulation, we uncomplicate our own lives.

I am the first to say I've lived both ways: knowing I should but ignoring those instincts (aka Holy Spirit convictions) and living with the consequences, and having the wisdom to do what I knew to be right. With the luxury of hindsight, I can testify that my life has gotten far less complicated since I realized that telling myself no was spiritual and that God has given me the authority as His child to be able to do it. Do not think because I haven't had an affair that it is because I haven't been tempted. I write about deleting messages because that is exactly what I have had to do in my own life when I've had contacts from people in the past that have made the hair on the back of my neck stand up. Do not think I didn't almost marry the wrong person. I had the wedding dress and all. And you already know about my shopping fast—a result of long-running self-indulgent yeses and finally, a no. Though I lived a successful self-told no in these areas with God's help, I have certainly lived without telling myself no in other ways, and it has led only to disaster.

This indulgent culture won't tell you that, or that your sin is not the boss of you, but the Bible will (Romans 6:6; Galatians 5:23–24). Knowledge alone is not what will save us in any of these circumstances I mentioned or a hundred more. It is not enough to know we should delete the message right away rather than entertain it. The Holy Spirit has to help us self-regulate in wisdom by running far, far away.

Trust me: we don't want the heartache.

4. The wise listen and are hungry to learn.

Every wise person I know is an astute observer. They watch. And by so doing, they take things in. There is a psychological reason why people have dedicated jobs to studying the body language of others—because so much is said without the sound of a single word. A wise person knows that often the best teacher of life is found in living it and the best lesson learned about people is in watching them live their lives—seeing their daily habits and patterns.

A wise person also listens. There is so much wisdom in listening, yet it is curiously loud in the world, with all of us overtalking each other. Rather than sit and listen to how the other feels, we often tell each other how we *should* feel. There is absolutely a time to speak, and in our acting out of the knowledge of the Word and self-regulation by the control and power of the Holy Spirit, we will know what and when that is. But listening also takes a level of discipline that many of us do not possess. We learn when we listen. We miss out when we don't.

A wise person also asks questions. I've talked in previous writings about my experience of going to counseling some years back for the first time. I thought then that the counselor was going to change me with his intelligent insights into my life, using all his book smarts from earned degrees when, in fact, it was something much simpler: his good questions got me to go to the core of who I am, how I feel, what I want, and my great struggle. (In some cases earned degrees do teach you the art of asking good questions but so does raw human interest.) It has been the hard or pointed questions people have asked me that have been the most change-producing catalysts for me, forcing me to take my own inventory. And on the flip side, asking others questions about their lives, their experiences, what they know and feel and think, has profoundly changed me as well. It has made me stop assuming so much and to instead develop greater empathy. We do ourselves a massive favor when, instead of reacting, we watch, listen, and ask questions, which is exactly what a wise person will do.

5. The wise take their representation seriously.

The idea that we represent the Lord Jesus Christ should never escape us. It should be the first thing we think about when we wake up and the last thing we think about when we go to bed. Life demands much of us, and many days we don't give this much of a thought. But it's what we have given our life to if we've given our life to Him. We can go our whole lives with this information and even be grateful for the information—that we are His, and that we will one day be in heaven with Him— but to remember our bond on a daily basis and honor it by the way we live is to live with the wisdom of the gospel, showing we understand our "bondservant" status (1 Corinthians 7:22 ESV).

Without Jesus, none of us can truly be wise. So even as we exercise the choice of wisdom over knowledge, we do so with the understanding and agreement of Proverbs 3:7–8:

> Be not wise in your own eyes;
>> fear the LORD, and turn away from evil.
> It will be healing to your flesh
>> and refreshment to your bones. (ESV)

GO TO GOD

Listening to the wrong people often leads to trouble.

King Hanun of the Ammonites learned this the hard way after his father died and King David made a sincere attempt at friendship by sending his ambassadors to the land of Ammon to offer his condolences. (See 2 Samuel 10.) I'll fast-track you through the story and spare you some of the cheeky details (literally), but the long and short of it is that due to wrong assumptions and bad advice on the part of Hanun's advisors when, in fact, David's motives had been pure, things went in a ditch. Wrong assumptions led to bad advice, which led to a battle between the powerful Israelites and the Ammonites, who were so afraid of their competition that they hired twenty thousand Aramean troops to help them and they were still defeated, anyway.

All because King Hanun listened to bad counsel.

Scroll through social media for very long and you'll see pieces of sermons in memes, in links, and in posts. You can get your daily dose of inspiration one hundred times over if you want it and never have to crack open the Word. I'm drawn to it too. I love words, and I love counsel. I love being able to share with people what I am learning as well. But are we getting anywhere? Maybe the beginning of wisdom for each of us is to ask ourselves this question, even now: Who and what influences me the most? If the answer is anything other than Jesus and the Word, we are face-to-face with something in dire need of adjustment. We can know more than other people and feel good about our intelligence and ability to articulate things and draw other people to our point of view, but how wise are we, really, if we are attempting to be a substitute for the wisdom of God in someone's life? And we can feel as if we are feeding our spiritual life by continually soaking in the thoughts and ideas of other folks, but if we are not first and foremost seeking spiritual nourishment from the root of all insight and under-standing, we are settling for secondhand. God can and does use us to communicate His truth. But it's forever going to be the best decision to go straight to the source Himself.

We will never go wrong by going to God with everything, but we could go wrong putting our faith in the counsel of the wisest man. If there's a choice to be made, always go to God.

And always, *always* choose wisdom over knowledge.

NINE

COMMITMENT
OVER MOOD

TEACH ME THAT IF I DO NOT LIVE A LIFE THAT SATISFIES
THEE, I SHALL NOT LIVE A LIFE THAT WILL SATISFY MYSELF.
—FROM *THE VALLEY OF VISION: A COLLECTION
OF PURITAN PRAYERS AND DEVOTIONS*

The only thing worse than being unwell is being unwell one
more day.

I say this to my husband when he talks to me about some things he
wants to work on because both of us have lived long enough to know
that speaking truth into a situation is the only way out. Heart sickness
can't thrive under exposure. It's only brave in the dark.

While I'm on the subject of getting well, did I tell you I got a desk
bike? It may be the best purchase I've made in years. My husband was a
skeptic for good reason, with the treadmill I just had to have a few years
ago collecting dust in the bonus room upstairs. But this is different.
I'm not on an exercise or weight loss kick this time. My legs had started
to become achy and sore with all the sitting, writing, and podcasting

I was doing, sometimes for ten to twelve hours a day, and I began to become concerned about things like a pulmonary embolism—not too far-fetched since my grandmother died from one. So I got scared into exercising, I guess you could say.

Sometimes the fear of something will drive you to a commitment, and it may be the best possible way a new lifestyle starts.

Most of us have the right idea about commitment—we want to do it for the right reasons and we resist it until those reasons seem right. But discernment amid our human nature is tricky, and, for many of us, waiting for "right" keeps us waiting most of our lives. In an ideal, unfallen world, we would do everything for the right reason and move forward under that umbrella at the exact right time. But since we don't know all and can't see all and we tend to do right in our own eyes (yes, even we who pray and seek God with our whole hearts because of our flesh), we cannot simply rely on what we determine is the right and best time to commit to something.

It is a false idea that commitment is more than a choice. If we wait for a feeling, we will likely wait too long or jump into something too soon. There's a reason Moses says in Deuteronomy 30 that choosing life is choosing to love, obey. and commit to God. There's no mention of waiting until it feels right or we are in the spiritual mood.

> Discernment amid our human nature is tricky, and, for many of us, waiting for "right" keeps us waiting most of our lives.

We don't typically use the word *mood* to define spiritual commitment, but when our decision to

- spend time in the Word versus spend time on our phone,
- seek God or seek advice from a friend when we have an issue,
- react instead of being disciplined enough to pause, or
- sit back and soak in spiritual things rather than get out and serve

is based on how we feel at that moment, it is a fair qualification. Mood is a temporary state of mind we can go in and out of, often determined by what's happening in front of us (which limits us because we cannot know and see what God does, 1 Corinthians 2:11) and requires trusting ourselves (which is foolish, according to Proverbs 28:26). If we are offended by the thought that mood could be determining the depth of our spiritual life, maybe it is because it feels painfully true.

It's not just that allowing our mood to dictate our life is spiritually unwise for the sake of our relationship with Jesus; it is also that it does us no favor for ourselves. Living mood-dependent has turned us into unfulfilled people. Not having to stick to anything *if we don't feel like it* leaves us never knowing the joy of finishing well and the strength of doing hard things. We live in a half-done society because when people are only halfway in, they tend to bail on things that don't feel good. I am not a proponent for denial of feelings—they are God-given and in many ways are meant to indicate what is happening in the deeper parts of a soul that need to be addressed. But being driven by them in decision-making as a general way of life can be dangerous. Ask anyone who has lived life driven by their moods, and they will tell you that it has led them astray ten times over and severely complicated life:

- the woman led by the thrill of an affair that wrecked an entire family
- the man whose job wasn't "fun" anymore, so he left it for another job, then another, and another, causing him a life of instability
- the teenager who bought into societal pressure to fit in and sent just that one nude picture to someone who said it was safe and regretfully watched it spread all over the Internet
- the person who wanted to just relax with a pill or a quick smoke, here and there, and became an unintentional addict

Unhealthy. Unwise and consequently painful. Complicating the already challenging day-to-day reality in which we all live.

On the other hand, choosing to live committed, no matter how or why it starts, uncomplicates a life. Because, for the believer, commitment is the choice to do it Jesus' way under any circumstance. And with the Bible telling us what that is, it makes things very cut-and-dried. I don't know about you, but in this confusing world I like simple instructions.

> Not having to stick to anything *if we don't feel like it* leaves us never knowing the joy of finishing well and the strength of doing hard things.

The question then to consider right now is this: Do I want my life more complicated than it is already, or will I commit to a Jesus-over-everything life, where He will "make known to me the path of life; in [His] presence there is fullness of joy; at [His] right hand are pleasures forevermore" (Psalm 16:11 ESV)?

I know, personally, which sounds better.

KEPT

Assuming you've already made a true *first things first* commitment to follow Jesus by way of salvation, the commitment that comes next is to immerse yourself in prayer and the Word and come under the constant influence of the Holy Spirit, and under *those* terms make daily decisions. Satan makes the process of following Jesus seem far more daunting than it is, so we are afraid to dive in with our whole hearts. We feel defeated before we start, which is his goal, to get us to never start. The converse of this lie about the Christian life being out of our grasp is true. When our lifestyle is driven by a Jesus-over-everything baseline commitment, decisions become less hard to make. The litmus test becomes His endorsement. We become kept by our commitment to give Jesus the priority in our lives, and commitment keeps us when realities of our humanity (fatigue, lust, anger, jealousy, resentment, fear) threaten to dictate right choices in life.

Consider Psalm 121 if you are skeptical about this idea:

> I lift up my eyes to the hills.
>> From where does my help come?
> My help comes from the LORD,
>> who made heaven and earth.
>
> He will not let your foot be moved;
>> he who keeps you will not slumber.
> Behold, he who keeps Israel
>> will neither slumber nor sleep.
>
> The LORD is your keeper;
>> the LORD is your shade on your right hand.
> The sun shall not strike you by day,
>> nor the moon by night.
>
> The LORD will keep you from all evil;
>> he will keep your life.
> The LORD will keep
>> your going out and your coming in
>> from this time forth and forevermore. (ESV)

The Lord is your keeper. I can't come up with a more comforting promise than that. Someone needs His relief right now. Someone needs His protection. Someone needs to know that while she goes to bed and falls asleep troubled by her many burdens of life, God stays awake and watches her with love. I am that someone. So are you. I don't trust my mood to run my life anymore. But I do trust God, or at least I want to.

Trust is hard for me, but the idea of being kept is so appealing it's made me dive in even more. I've been turning to 1 Peter 1:3–5 in light of this promise that if I choose commitment to God over my mood, the benefit will be His keeping of me:

> Blessed be the God and Father of our Lord Jesus Christ, who according to His abundant mercy has begotten us again to a living hope through the resurrection of Jesus Christ from the dead, to an inheritance incorruptible and undefiled and that does not fade away, reserved in heaven for you, who are kept by the power of God through faith for salvation ready to be revealed in the last time. (NKJV)

The keeping here is really twofold: an inheritance of eternity with Christ that is waiting for us as His children in heaven, and the keeping of us in the interim. As we journey through this life, we do not do so without His help and hope, for a good Father wouldn't have an inheritance awaiting people He wouldn't guide to it in the meantime. There would be no point, and God always has purpose in any and everything He does. This speaks to why He corrects us and why His standard does not just allow us to do things that we feel at the time. He knows that for us to enjoy what only He knows is awaiting us, He must actively father us in the process.[1]

I love what Milton Vincent says as to why gospel living is not a one and done but an ongoing, daily commitment and process:

> God did not give us His gospel just so we could embrace it and be converted. Actually, He offers it to us every day as a gift that keeps on giving to us everything we need for life and godliness. The wise believer learns this truth early and becomes proficient in extracting available benefits by being absorbed in the gospel, speaking it to ourselves when necessary, and by daring to reckon it true in all we do.[2]

We have nothing to do with God's gift of salvation and everything to do with the acceptance of it and the ongoing process of growing our faith. And yet in that there is choice and free will. The promise of eternity does not waver based on our poor decisions after salvation, but the keeping of our minds, bodies, and souls is a choice-by-choice partnership with Christ. My pastor, Jay Stewart, recently spoke something powerful and profound over us one Sunday that crystallizes this point: "What's better—to be able to say, 'I am forgiven and saved' or 'I have become like Christ?'" We can get technical about this and argue about how salvation is the most important thing, and on the core premise, I will agree. Nothing matters if we don't first choose to follow Christ. But to rest on our status of heaven-bound rather than pursue holiness and sanctification (the process of becoming like Christ) exposes our desire for a lazy faith. God's plan is not for us to accept salvation and sit with it. It is for us to share its miracle with the world.

> **God's plan is not for us to accept salvation and sit with it. It is for us to share its miracle with the world.**

To be kept is to be held or retained in one's possession, in order to provide support and structure.[3] These are all the things Jesus does for us in our daily commitment to Him. Even while living in this fallen world with pain and unwelcome surprises. Despite losses and rejection and the trouble that John 16:33 suggests this world brings. So many precious verses in the Word speak to the beautiful keeping of God in our daily lives—the choice of commitment over mood is the choice to stabilize ourselves *in the midst of*. We become a boat that is anchored, where, otherwise, we are tossed about by the waves. Waves and wind and rain still come. But we are kept by God in its fury.

We can believe this if we believe the Bible because it tells us so over and over again. We commit to a lifestyle of Jesus over everything, and He keeps us. What does that mean for us?[4]

- God Protects Us

  "And I tell you, you are Peter, and on this rock I will build my church, and the gates of hell shall not prevail against it." (Matthew 16:18)

  But the Lord is faithful. He will establish you and guard you against the evil one. (2 Thessalonians 3:3)

  > "My God, my rock, in whom I take refuge,
  > my shield, and the horn of my salvation,
  >   my stronghold and my refuge,
  >   my savior; you save me from violence.
  > I call upon the LORD, who is worthy to be praised,
  >   and I am saved from my enemies." (2 Samuel 22:3–4)

  > "Fear not, for I am with you;
  >   be not dismayed, for I am your God;
  > I will strengthen you, I will help you,
  >   I will uphold you with my righteous right hand." (Isaiah 41:10)

  > "No weapon that is fashioned against you shall succeed,
  >   and you shall refute every tongue that rises against you in
  >   judgment.
  > This is the heritage of the servants of the LORD
  >   and their vindication from me, declares the LORD."
  >   (Isaiah 54:17)

  > God is our refuge and strength,
  >   a very present help in trouble. (Psalm 46:1)

  > He who dwells in the shelter of the Most High
  >   will abide in the shadow of the Almighty.

I will say to the LORD, "My refuge and my fortress,
    my God, in whom I trust."
For he will deliver you from the snare of the fowler
    and from the deadly pestilence. (Psalm 91:1–3)
We know that everyone who has been born of God does not keep on sinning, but he who was born of God protects him, and the evil one does not touch him. (1 John 5:18)

- God Stays with Us

"Behold, I am with you always, to the end of the age." (Matthew 28:20)

But you are a chosen race, a royal priesthood, a holy nation, a people for his own possession, that you may proclaim the excellencies of him who called you out of darkness into his marvelous light. (1 Peter 2:9)

He has said, "I will never leave you nor forsake you." (Hebrews 13:5)

- God Works All Things for Our Good

And we know that for those who love God all things work together for good, for those who are called according to his purpose. (Romans 8:28)

In him we have obtained an inheritance, having been predestined according to the purpose of him who works all things according to the counsel of his will. (Ephesians 1:11)

"At that time shall arise Michael, the great prince who has charge of your people. And there shall be a time of trouble, such as never has been since there was a nation till that time.

But at that time your people shall be delivered, everyone whose name shall be found written in the book." (Daniel 12:1)

Though I walk in the midst of trouble,
    you preserve my life;
you stretch out your hand against the wrath of my enemies,
    and your right hand delivers me. (Psalm 138:7)

I don't know if in your life you've ever truly felt protected or safe. Maybe you have a history of people not sticking around, and you are the one who feels like it works out for everyone else but never for you. I won't talk you out of those feelings because you probably have good reason for the way you feel. The world is full of harmers, charmers, liars, and cheats. People win who don't deserve it. I'll never like any of this, and you don't have to either.

But these are all the more reason to make a commitment to the One whom we can trust with our whole heart. The One who protects us in our storms, stays with us when others take a walk, and gives us purpose for our lives. When you put it that way, it seems crazy to choose anyone or anything else.

OBEDIENCE

We can't talk about commitment without talking about obedience. For the believer in Jesus, the decision to follow Christ is a salvation-to-eternity commitment.

And we can't talk about obedience without talking about Abraham, our biblical hero-in-residence, perhaps best known for the near slaying of his son at God's request, for no reason apparent to Abraham. Except God *did* have His reason—even perhaps to show us the importance of obedience every time we read Genesis 22.

But what we sometimes forget when we recall this wild, incredible story is that Abraham didn't step into Genesis 22 a newbie. This was not his first rodeo with keeping his commitment to God in lieu of doing what he wanted.

There were many moments leading up to that memorable I'm-about-to-sacrifice-my-only-son-because-God-told-me-to moment, and they all involved Abraham obeying God. Abraham was obviously an amazing man, but no one is going to be ready for such an enormous task without some serious practice. You can't be prepared for a moment like this, a moment that involves a very large knife and your only son. You can, however, grow accustomed to a lifestyle that makes such a moment even possible. This is why a daily choice of commitment over mood is not only how you live a Jesus-over-everything life, but it's what helps you choose well in the bigger and more important daily life decisions—it creates spiritual muscle memory on which you can draw.

All the moments of Abraham's life had led him to *the* moment when he would make his mark as arguably the most loyal follower of God who ever lived.

Defining moments happen for all of us—they are the red dots on our memory time line, enmeshed in everyday life and preparing us for what's to come. We forget about most things—what we wore yesterday, what we ate for dinner two days ago. But not those defining moments; their scent lingers. We put those in the keepsake box, pull them out to talk about when we need someone to know what shaped us. But defining moments typically don't happen alone. They happen because other moments happened and led us to a place or time where we would otherwise not be. In that way the little moments that go unnoticed define the larger happenings of our lives.

Abraham's famous defining moment in Genesis 22 nearly eclipsed a life that had established plenty of previous credibility. He was in the habit of being committed to God. He had chosen the Lord over everything when it meant leaving all that he knew for an unknown future, moving from Ur to Haran and eventually to Canaan. He camped where God told him to camp. Moved when God told him to move. Believed when God said he would have a son with Sarah at age one hundred. This obedience came from a deep, committed relationship between Abraham and God, not based on circumstances or mood. Few of the things God asked of Abraham were desirable, but they were all preparatory.

Each step of obedience involved a great deal of trust by Abraham in His God. Early on, he had gotten used to the idea that God was in charge, which is why for us, the sooner we accept the preeminence of God that we talked about in chapter 1, the more settled our life becomes. With each encounter, God chipped away at Abraham's selfishness and proved Himself worthy of his trust. In turn, this formed Abraham's commitment to God, a commitment that held fast until he died at age 175 a very rich man in every way.

Abraham is a perfect example of a powerful truth: commitments will keep you when your mood (preference, will, desire) wants to pull you away. I can't imagine Abraham was in the mood to do any of the things God asked him to do over the years, but still, he did them. His life was the combination of many powerful and smaller, less eventful moments—all of which God used to make a difference in the end.

> Commitments will keep you when your mood (preference, will, desire) wants to pull you away.

Moments matter to God because He is in them all, and one moment can change everything in our life: The moment a child is born. The moment we get the bad news or scary health diagnosis. The moment you meet the person who becomes your lifelong best friend.

But moments with less fanfare matter just as much: The moment we decide we are done living below our potential, in the quiet of our bedroom one night, just us and God. The moment we send a text that seems like nothing to us but says just the right something to start someone else on a different path. The moment we decide we aren't going to be unwell anymore and buy the desk bike. Defining moments aren't all packaged in the highlighted moments others see, yet they can equally change our life.

A major sign we are choosing commitment over mood and living a Jesus-over-everything life in this area will be our visible spiritual transformation. It is as Bible teacher and author Beth Moore recently said: "The objective of all obedience to God is Christlikeness. God is conforming us into the image of His Son. If in our pursuit and practice of obedience, we look, act, talk and love less and less and less like Jesus, something has gone awry."[5] We can preach Jesus and live the opposite, but everyone will write us off.

I talk with plenty of frustrated believers who want a close relationship with God and they aren't sure why they can't seem to get there. They go to conferences, attend church, do Bible studies with friends, and read their Bibles regularly. Yet nothing ever seems to stick. It's a familiar place for a lot of us, and we want to change it, but we don't know how. Could it be because we look at the gospel as a to-do rather than a lifestyle, so we don't understand the way it is meant to truly transform us? We don't know how much we could love the way the Bible could change us if we would give it time to take root.

God has been showing me recently how much I allow my feelings to get in the way of His Word in my life and what He wants me to do, and how that becomes my own hindrance. Too often I trust and follow my feelings over God; too often I'm driven by society's expectations or influence or by my own preferences when I'm in a selfish mind-set, which is a daily struggle, in fact.

And I know I'm not alone. Society feeds into this tendency to follow our feelings over our commitments. If I am too tired to show up for a party one night, I just text the host, and I know she will understand, or maybe I don't text her. I just don't show, and it's not a big deal. We all offer a pass for a busy or stressed-out life because we know that eventually we will need the same pass. I want to be more committed than I am, but so often I skip out simply because I'm not in the mood to do something. I just don't *feel* like it. If we are looking for support, we can find it, even with memes on Instagram that will give us permission to bail. But that can complicate things because with every excuse for the things we don't feel like doing comes the price of having to make up a lie or face someone we broke a promise to or earn back our reputation and prove that we really aren't a flake. We shouldn't live under the burden of people's expectations, but we have gone so far the other way in the name of our rights that we have disregarded personal courtesy, integrity, and the good reputation that commitment is all about.

Commitment is a rare thing, so when we choose it, we should expect to seem rare. In the faith sense it's the Luke 9:23 command played out: the denial of self to take up our individual crosses and follow Jesus. Perhaps that is why we find it so precious when we see someone who is truly committed, in spite of their feelings or circumstances. It's also why the prosperity gospel is offensive to those of us who disbelieve it, and we bristle at its suggestion that Jesus wants us to be rich and famous—if you read the Word, it rings hollow and is biblically untrue.

I don't believe in a prosperity gospel. I believe in an obedience gospel. Not because I don't believe Jesus loves me and wants good things for me or because I wish for a prettier way to do this life, but because I must live in the reality of what is. Prosperity gospel tells us exactly what we want to hear, so in our flesh we won't tire of it. Yet it provides none of the true strength commitment does. The Father has great love for us, but He's not about our comfort; He's about our transformation. He cares deeply about our hurts and, yes, even our desires but only within the context and understanding that our will is already dead (John 3:30). We die in order to live. And in that death to our preferences, Jesus owns the emotional real estate of our life.

My own life has been marked by defining moments, both seen

and unseen, and in the ones that have been most fruitful, God has first tamed a will that once ran astray. The defining moment I gave my heart to Jesus, at six years old, after a Sunday night at church. The defining moment I drove home from college in the snow to come clean to my mother about the reckless way I had been living. The defining moment fewer than ten years ago when I lay with my face on the fibers of my office carpet and told God I would stop running from His call on my life and do whatever He said.

And then, sometimes, the defining moments have been fleshly choices leading to years of regretful repercussions. Growing up, the choice to lie to my parents about relationships and whereabouts and things I was doing over and over again. The choice to abuse my body through restricting calories and overexercising to stay impossibly thin. The choice to drown my feelings in shopping instead of turning to God. Putting Jesus first has never come naturally to me. It comes hard, tearfully, and typically only when I find myself backed into a repentant corner.

Commitment over mood isn't a slogan or a trite cliché. It's a hard-fought death to self. It's seeing the feelings for the idols that they are in our lives, recognizing the times that we've put them over the call of the gospel, and then making the decision to choose Jesus over everything. Possible, while purposeful.

And rest assured throughout, God will continue to be relentless in His pursuit of heart cleaning. It's the only thing He wants. Mood won't drive us to live a James 1:27 life—caring for widows and orphans is not easy work. Mood isn't enough to propel us to a life mission of cross-carrying. We can be great church attenders, but we will never be powerful kingdom influencers if we are ruled by our moods. We'll have no consistency in our relationship with Him if we're swayed by every fleeting feeling.

God uses the moments of our life to chisel us, even in ways we can't see, so that we might be ready for that *big* moment, the one moment that will require more of us than most of us are ready for right now. We may not wish for it, but a loving God loves us enough not to leave us in our selfish life.

Abraham's moment is big and Bible famous now, but it was personal at the time. Whatever your journey looks like, you can count on it being personal too. What all of us want is to be prepared to say yes to absolutely anything God asks, however we get there, and I'm not sure if any of our roads to get there will ever look exactly like we think.

There's no contest or scale—commitment is a hard-fought decision to obey and trust God, staying with Him no matter what the moments look like, believing it is the journey that shapes us into the people God wants us to be.

In life
    faith will be tested,
    God can be trusted, and
    our commitments will keep us when our moods want to
        pull us away.

TEN

JESUS OVER EVERYTHING: HOME

AS GOD IS EXALTED TO THE RIGHT PLACE
IN OUR LIVES, A THOUSAND PROBLEMS
ARE SOLVED ALL AT ONCE.[1]
—A. W. TOZER

I'm writing this last chapter from inside a beautiful ranch home in remote Texas, with its immaculate floors and majestic beams, a gourmet kitchen newly redone, and enough space to house a family reunion.

But walk outside and the Texas heat will accost you, suck the breath right out of your lungs. Cacti stand guard at every turn, begging you to get too close and let them prove themselves. When my mom and I drove through the ranch's big iron gates yesterday, our van nearly got run over by a determined deer. "If we go walking, I'll give you some boots in case of rattlesnakes," Mom said as we pulled up to the front.

Welcome, and by the way . . . beware.

Mom married bonus dad, John, nine months ago, so they are

still newlyweds. "Old newlyweds," Mom points out in her typical self-effacing style, and at seventy-five (and he's seventy-eight), she's not wrong. John owns the ranch and has for years, and this is my first time coming. It's an eclectic blend of real rattlesnake skins from goners who slid across the porch to their demise, poacher guns from Africa on the wall, Bible verses in fancy carved wood plaques, and Pottery Barn rugs. There's a Walmart not too far away but no Internet. Fancy sconces adorn the walls while a mouse makes his home in the bed I planned to sleep in last night. (No further comment on that situation.)

"This place is hazardous," I tell Mom after she warns me about some spiky plants on the porch I need to watch out for, and she nods.

"John says everything around here either sticks you, pricks you, stings you, or bites you."

I make a mental note.

I've come here to write, though I'm not altogether sure at the moment why. As a pragmatist writer, spending the money to fly somewhere, even a free place, always seems like a luxury I didn't need to get inspiration—or maybe that's what I tell myself so I don't have to bother with the inconvenience of travel. It doesn't take me long to understand why Jesus might have nudged this scenario for creative expression.

John loves to ride the land at night, and I soon see why. We hop into his decked-out camo Gator, binoculars in hand, only one of us a pretend rancher. "I need to see a rattlesnake and a bobcat, please," I say, like I'm ordering off the menu, and John grins. He loves sharing his love for this land and the animals that roam it. Javelinas, deer, quail, hawks, and at least a million rabbits come into my sights, and I feel like a giddy GI Jane taking them all in.

"This is God's land. He made it all. It's all His," John says to no one in particular. I recognize that faraway look. I saw my dad get it when he would talk about God's country too. There's something about being out in nature that helps you remember that everything is truly His.

All this Texas land, all around me, as far as the eye can see, takes me back to the words I wrote in chapter 1, at home in a twelve-by-fifteen air-conditioned office in suburbia. Here on the ranch, now an actual visual for me of the land of the deadly overs with its hazards and hidden danger underfoot, I get to experience firsthand what I wrote about weeks ago. It's a tangible reminder of a song I used to sing as a kid— "He's got the whole world in His hands"—and Genesis 1, the most prolific example of how from then until forever, Jesus is over everything.

In the beginning, God created the heavens and the earth. The earth was without form and void, and darkness was over the face of the deep. . . .

And God said, "Let there be light," and there was light. . . . And there was evening and there was morning, the first day.

And God said, "Let there be an expanse in the midst of the waters. . . . And there was evening and there was morning, the second day.

And God said, "Let the waters under the heavens be gathered together into one place, and let the dry land appear." And it was so. . . .

And God said, "Let the earth sprout vegetation, plants yielding seed, and fruit trees bearing fruit in which is their seed, each according to its kind, on the earth." And it was so. . . . And there was evening and there was morning, the third day.

And God said, "Let there be lights in the expanse of the heavens to separate the day from the night. . . . And there was evening and there was morning, the fourth day.

And God said, "Let the waters swarm with swarms of living creatures, and let birds fly above the earth across the expanse of the heavens." . . . And there was evening and there was morning, the fifth day.

And God said, "Let the earth bring forth living creatures according to their kinds. . . ."

Then God said, "Let us make man in our image, after our likeness. And let them have dominion over the fish of the sea and over the birds of the heavens and over the livestock and over all the earth and over every creeping thing that creeps on the earth."

So God created man in his own image,
in the image of God he created him;
male and female he created them. (vv. 1–27 ESV)

Sometimes we just need to go back to the basics and remember where it all came from. Whether or not we put Jesus over everything in our lives, He *is* over everything now and forevermore—the land, the government, the world, us. Ephesians 1:19–22 affirms this truth. I don't want us to get so heady over the whole thing, worried about our responsibility in this, that we forget the richness of the reality of Jesus, first—the beautiful benefit of being covered by God. Because, in the end, remembering how good Jesus is to us will motivate us to want to put Jesus first. Jesus over our hurts. Jesus over our successes. Jesus over all this mess down here on earth that doesn't make sense. He is covering us, holding us, sheltering us from being overcome by it all like a protective awning. Jesus over everything—God is with us; the Father covers us; Jesus *has* us. Psalm 91 says it so well:

Whoever dwells in the shelter of the Most High
will rest in the shadow of the Almighty.
I will say of the LORD, "He is my refuge and my fortress,
my God, in whom I trust.

Surely he will save you
from the fowler's snare
and from the deadly pestilence.

> He will cover you with his feathers,
>> and under his wings you will find refuge;
>> his faithfulness will be your shield and rampart.
>
> (vv. 1–4 NIV)

Jesus over everything is a call and a Colossians 1 responsibility, but it's equally an Ephesians 1 reality to daily let soak in deep. It's a requirement with sweet and abiding benefit to our soul. When Jesus asks us to put Him first, it's out of His great love for us to let Him do the heavy lifting. Has life gotten hard for you, friend? Has it gotten complicated? Then let Jesus have it. Let Him manage it. He can sort out the mess.

You and I are so much more than a professional bio, level of achievement, relationship status, financial state, or top or bottom of someone's list, so let's not sell ourselves short. *Have you fought hard to stay with Jesus? Do you have the bruises to prove it?* These are the important things. Putting Him first won't always be easy, but it will be worth it. The true success of a person is not in whether she can make her life work; it's in whether she can die to her life enough for Jesus to work in her. When hard times come, how much we've practiced this principle will show.

> **The true success of a person is not in whether she can make her life work; it's in whether she can die to her life enough for Jesus to work in her.**

The things we've talked about in this book—daily choices of the Jesus-over-everything life—are the practices that sow into our own growth. If we've been looking to grow closer to Jesus, these eight choices are the way. If we've wanted to uncomplicate our lives and help create inside of us both character and fortitude to stand in these tough times, these priorities will do it:

Real over pretty: When we want to look perfect, we fight to be ourselves.

Love over judgment: When we feel judgmental, we
   choose love.

Holiness over freedom: When we could say yes but it won't
   make us more like Jesus, we say no instead.

Service over spotlight: When we want attention, we lift up
   someone else.

Steady over hype: When the world tries to influence us, we
   continually go to the Word.

Honesty over hiding: When we want to lie, we out the secret
   to take away its power.

Wisdom over knowledge: When we are tempted to rely on
   books or outside inspiration to be our best teacher, we ask
   God to make us wise instead.

Commitment over mood: When we want to run, we stay.

These are the ways we live a Jesus-over-everything life—not by
might or will or desire but by choosing the right *overs* in everyday
situations that come up.

It is the way we help give ourselves the simpler life we crave—
choice by choice, moment by moment, day by day.

IT'S ALL HIS

My friend Kristin Lemus has been studying about land in Scripture too.
In her studies she's found that land is given to steward the fruit thereof
and as a good inheritance, and it typically manifests as a *promise* long
before the *possession* of it takes place. I find this to be beautifully true.
God's promises, time and again, are for the possession of heart desires.
Healing and hope, relief and fulfillment—a peaceful life instead of the
complicated one we currently live—are graciously offered by Him yet
dependent upon us. In that way we often long for things we can have if

we will do our life God's way. So in order to have the life we want, we must do *the* one thing: decide we want to live the Jesus-over-everything life and work that choice by exercising the daily disciplines these chapters thoroughly talk about. These are the things that Jesus lived and died for, and as we also live and die for them, we find our truest identity.

So, you see, putting Jesus over everything isn't the real struggle. That will happen naturally with a mind-set change—realizing that it is the way our life will work and not entertaining substitutes. When our mind-set changes, practices that were once difficult for us often become much less so. This is our truest struggle: wasting time on the way around Jesus being the only way by behaviors that temporarily mimic the joy and freedom only found in the priority of Christ. (Hello, shopping addiction. Remember that?) When we become convinced that putting Him first is the means to the simpler, joyful life, we will no longer run from it but will run to it for reprieve. Just as easily as we choose our way, the more we practice choosing Jesus, the more we get in the habit of Him being in first place.

But Kristin also reminds me that we often have to fight fiercely for our land. It can be captured, stolen, ruined, and become desolate. How well a lot of us know something about that. We have had parts of our life taken from us, ruined and tarnished, and some of that is not ours to own. Life has left some of us with trust issues, so trusting even Jesus with our life is a hard-fought choice. I don't know where you are with your Jesus-over-everything process or what reminder you need: to take possession of the promise, to choose what He chooses, to find comfort in His covering, or maybe just to remember the words of John in our ranch ride that day: "This is God's land. He made it all. It's all His." But all any of us really need to know is that life is found in Him.

> When we become convinced that putting Him first is the means to the simpler, joyful life, we will no longer run from it but will run to it for reprieve.

Then Jesus told his disciples, "If anyone would come after me, let him deny himself and take up his cross and follow me. For whoever would save his life will lose it, but whoever loses his life for my sake will find it. (Matthew 16:24–25 ESV)

It's now Friday, three days after I wrote the first part of this chapter while at the Texas ranch.

Mom and John and now my family who have joined us have driven some miles to a different Texas ranch, where snakes and bobcats live and, this time, a real longhorn and several visible scorpions too. I'm a long way from the simpler life of holding kittens for a living in Enid, Oklahoma—a long way from my office in North Carolina too. It's 110 degrees out today. Cacti are still taking their job seriously. A tarantula lies dead on the gravel, overbaked in the Texas sun, and none of us attended his funeral.

This ranch is gorgeous but lonely. It's way too far out to be found on a GPS—more like "follow the road until it curves left; then where you see that old red truck, turn right" kind of a vibe. (Then you'll still go two miles down a dusty road you aren't sure isn't leading you to nowhere.) After arrival and upon inspecting the exquisite furniture, trinkets, glass pots, and art inside (and turning on the AC, which winds up not working), we head outside to the loveliest of outdoor living spaces, so large a small church could have a gathering around its fountain center point. Things are dusty and mothy from lack of human presence, and one lone bat flies out to greet us, which no one is happy about. It's a beautiful place. People who love Jesus use it for good. But, in the end, it's still just a place. It is a place that will weather and age and collect dust and, apparently, bats too. Matthew 6:20 flashes into my brain: "But collect for yourselves treasures in heaven, where neither moth nor rust destroys, and where thieves don't break in and steal" (HCSB).

And I think about this life—how it rusts. How it collects dusts. How people steal from us. How when we are gone, there's nothing here we miss, and our stuff is relegated to trash bins and auctions.

How so much in our lives is precious yet how much of it is rubble and ash.

But in both God remains.

How it's all His.

How we're all His.

Jesus over everything.

From Genesis 1 until the end.

JESUS OVER EVERYTHING MANIFESTO

Real over Pretty: When we want to look perfect, we fight to be ourselves.

Love over Judgment: When we feel judgmental, we choose love.

Holiness over Freedom: When we could say yes but it won't make us more like Jesus, we say no instead.

Service over Spotlight: When we want attention, we lift up someone else.

Steady over Hype: When the world tries to influence us, we continually go to the Word.

Honesty over Hiding: When we want to lie, we out the secret to take away its power.

Wisdom over Knowledge: When we are tempted to rely on books or outside inspiration to be our best teacher, we ask God to make us wise instead.

Commitment over Mood: When we want to run, we stay.

ACKNOWLEDGMENTS

WITH ALL LOVE, HONOR, AND THANKS . . .

Scotty: Here we went, again—me, at my desk in compression socks with unwashed hair for days on end to complete this project, and you, assuring me it's okay that I didn't get around to making dinner yet again. I know being married to a writer isn't easy, especially this one. You know my weak spots, but you've never outed me. You keep me laughing and force me to take compliments. I'm Linus, and you're my blanket. I love you.

Graham, Micah, and Shae: Everything important I wrote down for you in these pages. (Since I am not disciplined enough to journal, can this count?) I've gotten a lot wrong as a person and as your mom, but I hope you'll be able to say about me one day from personal experience: "She loved Jesus more than anything." I sure have loved getting to love you, my deepest joys and now almost-grown best friends.

Mom: I know that some of what I write in this book isn't easy to read. I also know you will accept the words with the same grace and love with which you have always accepted me. Thank you for taking care of my heart your whole life. You put Jesus first. If legacy can truly be passed down, it is the one you have left with me. May He bless you, sweetest woman, momma, and friend.

Dianne and Richard Whittle: I truly have the greatest in-laws on the planet. You are both better to me than I deserve, and I honor you for being faithful parents, business owners, church members, neighbors, friends, and (the most incredible) grandparents all these years. Your generosity has had reach far beyond what you could ever know. I have heard every single cheer you have thrown up for me in my ministry and as a mother and wife, and it has made my heart soar. Thank you. I love you both deeply.

Lisa Jackson: Sometimes you don't realize you need someone as much as you do until you have them, and then you wonder how you survived without them for this long. That, my friend, is how I feel about you. You will probably never know the healing our relationship has brought to places that sorely needed mending, but I suspect you are intuitive enough to sense it without words. I'm forever grateful I feel the safety and freedom not to have to couch anything with you. Thank you for a healthy working relationship, being crazy smart about literary things, and knowing my heart from day one and taking this leap with me. Can't wait to buy you dinner.

Megan Dobson: I knew from our breakfast that you were the one I wanted to help make me better, and you have. Thank you. This book needed you. So did I.

Renee and Paula: You've put in significant work here. Thank you for caring about this project and protecting its integrity from start to finish.

JOE Podcast listeners: You have my heart. That you would accept the invitation to listen, when you have so many other things you could do, is precious, and I hold it tender. In so many ways, this book is for you.

Support team: This part could really say—to basically everyone else in my life: my church, my friends, *you know who you are*—if we've briefly talked about JOE or you've prayed for me, you are my support team, and I thank you. But I have to name just a few people, specifically: Colleen, Angie, Alli, Caroline, Sharon, Myquillin, and

Wendy—these women know the roles they play in my life, what they mean to me, and how they've cheered for me. Caleb, Kathryn, and Josh: I truly could not do this work without you. And Sara Riemersma, my soul sister: Here's to more meaty, feisty Bible study shoots.

MY SAVIOR, JESUS CHRIST: I AM YOURS.

NOTES

CHAPTER 1: THE LAND OF THE DEADLY *OVERS*

1. Jill Carattini, "God of Possibility," *A Slice of Infinity*, accessed September 5, 2019, https://www.rzim.org/read/a-slice-of-infinity /god-of-possibility.
2. Kirsten Powers, "Why 'Thoughts and Prayers' Is Starting to Sound So Profane," *Washington Post*, November 6, 2017, https://www .washingtonpost.com/news/acts-of-faith/wp/2017/10/03/why -thoughts-and-prayers-is-starting-to-sound-so-profane/.
3. @Wearethatfamily, July 8, 2019, Instagram post.
4. Lore Wilbert, "Enough Beauty to Go Around," *Sayable* (blog), June 26, 2017, http://www.sayable.net/blog/2017/6/26/enough-beauty -to-go-around. Used by permission.
5. Quoted from my old, old, old copy of the 1996 version of the New Living Translation.

CHAPTER 2: REAL OVER PRETTY

1. All Luke Lang quotes in this book are used with permission.
2. Justin Taylor, "What Did Jesus Look Like?" Gospel Coalition, July 9, 2010, https://www.thegospelcoalition.org/blogs/justin-taylor/what -did-jesus-look-like/.
3. N. T. Wright, *After You Believe: Why Christian Character Matters* (San Francisco: HarperOne, 2012), 108.

NOTES

CHAPTER 3: LOVE OVER JUDGMENT

1. Wanda Sykes (@iamwandasykes), "Sobbing, missing my grandmother. Yeah, it's been 35 yrs, but, she loved me," Twitter, June 8, 2019, 10:48 p.m., https://twitter.com/iamwandasykes/status/1137597365731364865?.
2. C. S. Lewis, *The Four Loves* (repr.; San Francisco: HarperOne, 2017), 155–56.
3. Martin Luther King Jr., *Strength to Love* (New York: Harper & Row, 1963), 37.

CHAPTER 4: HOLINESS OVER FREEDOM

1. Lisa Bevere, *Adamant: Finding Truth in a Universe of Opinions* (Grand Rapids: Revell, 2018). Used by permission.
2. Os Guinness, *The Call* (Nashville, TN: Thomas Nelson, 2003), 157.
3. Lisa Whittle, *I Want God: Forever Changed by the Revival of Your Soul* (Eugene, OR: Harvest House, 2014), 172.
4. *Knowing Faith*, podcast, #32-"Christology and Creeds: The Doctrine of Christology," The Village Church Resources, February 21, 2019, https://www.tvcresources.net/resource-library/podcasts/32-christology-and-creeds-the-doctrine-of-christology.
5. Charles Haddon Spurgeon, "Moab Is My Wash Pot," *Metropolitan Tabernacle Pulpit* 16, no. 983 (1870), sermons in Modern English, http://www.spurgeongems.org/vols16-18/chs983.pdf.

CHAPTER 5: SERVICE OVER SPOTLIGHT

1. Phil Dooley (@PhillDooley), "The BEST teams are made up of a bunch of NOBODIES who love EVERYBODY & serve ANYBODY and DON'T care about becoming a SOMEBODY!," Twitter, February 3, 2014, 9:06 a.m., https://twitter.com/philldooley/status/430386825749082112.
2. Garrett Kell, "Stop Photobombing Jesus," Gospel Coalition, April 29, 2017, https://www.thegospelcoalition.org/article/stop-photobombing-jesus/.
3. Kronos Incorporated, "The Employee Burnout Crisis: Study Reveals

Big Workplace Challenge in 2017," Kronos, January 9, 2017, https://
www.kronos.com/about-us/newsroom/employee-burnout-crisis-study
-reveals-big-workplace-challenge-2017. See also Alexander Kunst,
"Percentage of Adults in the U.S. Who Very Often or Often
Experienced Select Stress and Burnout Symptoms as of February 2017,
by Burn-Out-Risk," Statista, last updated September 3, 2019, https://
www.statista.com/statistics/675797/often-or-very-often-felt-stress-or
-burnout-sypmtoms-adults-us-by-burn-out-risk/; Jenny Rough, "From
Moms to Medical Doctors, Burnout Is Everywhere These Days,"
Washington Post, March 30, 2019, https://www.washingtonpost.com
/national/health-science/from-moms-to-medical-doctors-burnout
-is-everywhere-these-days/2019/03/29/1cea7d92-401d-11e9-922c
-64d6b7840b82_story.html?.

CHAPTER 6: STEADY OVER HYPE

1. *Merriam-Webster*, s.v. "hype" (verb 2), accessed September 11, 2019,
   https://www.merriam-webster.com/dictionary/hype.
2. Ann Voskamp, *The Broken Way: A Daring Path into the Abundant Life*
   (Grand Rapids: Zondervan, 2016).
3. Eugene H. Peterson, *A Long Obedience in the Same Direction:
   Discipleship in an Instant Society*, 2nd ed. (Downers Grove, IL:
   InterVarsity, 2000), 16.

CHAPTER 7: HONESTY OVER HIDING

1. Carlos A. Rodriguez (@CarlosHappyNPO), "Don't pretend. Cry.
   Scream. Break a few things if you need to. God is not afraid of your
   darkness," Twitter, April 20, 2019, 6:28 a.m., https://twitter.com
   /CarlosHappyNPO/status/1119593682984931328. Used by permission.

CHAPTER 8: WISDOM OVER KNOWLEDGE

1. Voddie Bachum, "Expository Apologetics 101," video recording
   (37:29), January 21, 2016, Spiritual Life Conference (Spring 2016),
   Dallas Theological Seminary, https://voice.dts.edu/chapel/expository
   -apologetics-101-baucham-voddie/?adsource=TUBE_chapel.

2. Thayer and Smith, *The KJV New Testament Greek Lexicon*, s.v. "eido," accessed September 11, 2019, https://www.biblestudytools.com /lexicons/greek/kjv/eido.html.

3. Miles Kington, "Heading for a Sticky End," *Independent* (UK), March 28, 2003, https://www.independent.co.uk/voices/columnists /miles-kington/heading-for-a-sticky-end-112674.html.

CHAPTER 9: COMMITMENT OVER MOOD

1. See Andrew Murray, "Kept by the Power of God," Bible Study Tools, accessed September 11, 2019, https://www.biblestudytools.com /classics/murray-absolute-surrender/kept-by-the-power-of-god.html.

2. Milton Vincent, A *Gospel Primer for Christians: Learning to See the Glories of God's Love* (Bemidji, Minn.: FOCUS, 2011), 5.

3. See Dictionary.com, s.v. "kept," accessed September 11, 2019, https:// www.dictionary.com/browse/kept?s=t.

4. The following scriptures are taken from the ESV® Bible.

5. Beth Moore (@BethMooreLPM), "The objective of all obedience to God is Christlikeness. God is conforming us into the image of His Son. If in our pursuit and practice of obedience, we look, act, talk and love less and less and less like Jesus, something has gone awry," Twitter, May 9, 2019, 5:19 a.m., https://twitter.com/BethMooreLPM /status/1126461656190607360.

CHAPTER 10: JESUS OVER EVERYTHING: HOME

1. A. W. Tozer (@TozerAW), "As God is exalted to the right place in our lives, a thousand problems are solved all at once," Twitter, June 8, 2015, 10:30 a.m., https://twitter.com/tozeraw/status /607962865929101313.

ABOUT THE AUTHOR

LISA WHITTLE is the author of seven books, and her wit and bold bottom-line approach have made her a sought-after Bible teacher. She is also the creator of a companion video Bible study for *Jesus over Everything*. A pastor's daughter and longtime ministry leader in issues relevant to the church, Lisa is the founder of Ministry Strong and the popular *Jesus over Everything* podcast, which debuted in the top twenty-five of Christian podcasts. Her love runs deep to see people pursue Jesus for life, grow deep roots of faith, and walk strong in the midst of a world that so often seems to have gone crazy.

Lisa has done master's work in marriage and family counseling, advocated for Compassion International, and been featured on numerous media outlets through the years. She and her husband live in North Carolina with their three mostly grown children, who still come home for dinner.

New Video Study for Your Church or Small Group

If you've enjoyed this book, now you can go deeper with the companion video Bible study!

In this six-session video Bible study, Lisa Whittle helps you apply the principles in *Jesus over Everything* to your life. The study guide includes video notes, group discussion questions, and personal study and reflection materials for in-between sessions.

Study Guide
9780310118770

DVD
9780310118794

Available now at your favorite bookstore,
or streaming video on StudyGateway.com.

THOMAS NELSON
Since 1798